VISUAL QUICKSTART GUIDE

.MAC

David Reynolds

 **Peachpit Press**

Visual QuickStart Guide

.Mac
David Reynolds

Peachpit

1249 Eighth Street
Berkeley, CA 94710
510/524-2178
800/283-9444
510/524-2221 (fax)

Find us on the World Wide Web at: www.peachpit.com
To report errors, please send a note to errata@peachpit.com

Peachpit is a division of Pearson Education
Copyright © 2006 by David Reynolds

Editor: Nikki Echler McDonald
Production Editor: Simmy Cover
Copyeditor: Elissa Rabellino
Compositor: Sean McDonald
Indexer: FireCrystal Communications
Cover Design: The Visual Group
Cover Production: George Mattingly / GMD

ISBN 0-321-30473-X

9 8 7 6 5 4 3 2 1

Printed and bound in the United States of America

Dedication

This book is dedicated to my father, who made me a far better man than I would have been had I not known him.

Acknowledgments

I'd like to thank the following people, without whom... well, I shudder to think about it.

My wife Susan and sons Ben and Jake, for their tolerance and reminders about what really matters in life.

My good friend and excellent editor Nikki McDonald, who is a joy to work with—even if she does push me to be a better writer.

The good folks at Peachpit Press—Cliff Colby, Elissa Rabellino, Sean McDonald, Simmy Cover, Sara Jane Todd, Jackie Hill, Kim Becker and everyone else—who gave me this opportunity and who worked so hard to make a quality book.

TABLE OF CONTENTS

GETTING STARTED

Back at the turn of the millennium, Apple came out with a suite of Internet tools called iTools. This suite consisted of a mac.com e-mail address as well as KidSafe (a filter for child-friendly Web sites), HomePage (an easy-to-use tool for building Web sites), and iDisk (online storage that was accessible using just about any Internet connection). Apple's Internet strategy basically boiled down to a nifty set of Mac-only tools meant to make Mac users' lives a little easier.

Fast-forward five years. The tools are no longer free and the name has changed—iTools now goes by .Mac—but the goal remains the same: make Mac users' lives easier. With a "mac.com" e-mail address, iDisk, and HomePage still at its core, .Mac now also includes tight integration with Mac OS X, as well as a host of other features, all for just $99 a year.

Before you begin using your .Mac account, you'll want to set a few system preferences in Mac OS X. Setting these preferences now will make your .Mac account easier to use and more efficient in the long run. You'll only have to do it once, barring a few exceptions. You should, for example, change your account password every so often for security purposes, and you may need to update your credit card information occasionally. After all, who can resist six months at 0 percent APR?

In this chapter, I'll cover how to create your .Mac account, set your .Mac preferences, manage your .Mac account, and set up your iDisk.

GETTING STARTED

About .Mac

.Mac isn't just a single application or Web site. It's a suite of Internet services that's meant to help Mac users get more from their Macs. I'll quickly walk through each of the .Mac services now before going into greater detail on how to use each one later in the book.

- ◆ **.Mac Mail**—At the center of your .Mac membership is a full e-mail account ending in "@mac.com." This e-mail account can be used to send and receive e-mail on any computer that has a POP or IMAP client available, and that's pretty much every one out there. In addition, your .Mac account comes with a Web-based e-mail interface that lets you send and receive e-mail from any Web browser.

- ◆ **iDisk**—All .Mac accounts come with 250 MB of online storage in the form of an iDisk. Support for iDisk is built into Mac OS X, and using it is a lot like using any other network server—or even a hard drive, for that matter. iDisk serves as the backbone for publishing Web pages and synchronizing information between Macs.

- ◆ **HomePage**—Your .Mac membership includes HomePage, a handy piece of software that allows you to quickly build Web pages, such as photo albums, movie theaters, and file download pages. HomePage uses files that you upload to your iDisk. HomePage is also integrated with iPhoto, making it incredibly easy to share your pictures.

(continues on next page)

In Case You Don't Have a .Mac Account

If you've bought this book, we're assuming that you've taken the plunge and signed up for a .Mac account. Congratulations! It'll change your life.

If you're *browsing* this book, however, and you're contemplating a purchase, you might not yet have a .Mac account. Getting one is easy; all you need is a credit card, an Internet connection, and a Web browser.

To sign up as a .Mac member, visit www.mac.com and click the Join Now button on the front page. You'll be asked to provide a credit card number, preferred member name, billing address, password, and the like. Signing up is painless and takes only a few minutes. So what are you waiting for?

◆ **Backup**—Each .Mac membership comes with a copy of Backup, a free utility designed to automate data back-ups to your .Mac account as well as to CDs, DVDs, and other volumes. Making sure your important files get backed up doesn't sound very sexy, but when you're facing a corrupt hard drive and you don't have a backup, a free backup utility starts looking pretty good.

◆ **Address Book**—Your .Mac account lets you synchronize your Address Book data so that it's available to you anywhere you have access to a Web browser. And with Mac OS X 10.4 Tiger, you can share your Address Book with others.

◆ **iCards**—With a .Mac account, you can create and send e-mail greeting cards, either drawing from Apple's professionally designed assortment, or choosing from your own custom creations.

◆ **.Mac Sync**—With Mac OS X 10.4, you can synchronize important information, such as Keychain passwords, Mail's Smart Mailboxes, Safari bookmarks, and other data to your .Mac account—which lets you keep that information in sync with another Mac and provides you with a backup copy. Even those running Mac OS X 10.3 can use iSync to keep their information synchronized across Macs.

Hardware and Software Requirements

You don't need much to run .Mac—its requirements are pretty minimal. To run .Mac and use most of its features, all you need is a Macintosh running Mac OS X, 128 MB of RAM, and a browser such as Safari, Microsoft Internet Explorer 5 or later, or Netscape 7 or later. But if you want to use Backup 2—the free file backup software that comes with your .Mac account—you'll need Mac OS X 10.2.8 or later. To run iDisk, you'll need Mac OS X 10.1.2 or later. The iDisk Utility for Windows requires—you guessed it—a PC running Windows XP.

✔ Tip

■ You can find a full rundown of all .Mac system requirements at www.mac.com/1/systemrequirements.html.

Configuring Mac OS X

After you've bought and paid for your .Mac account, you could go to www.mac.com, log in, and begin using some features—such as Mail—right away. However, to get the most out of your .Mac account, you'll want to configure your Mac's operating system to work with it by setting up your .Mac preferences. After all, one of the chief benefits of having a .Mac account is its tight integration with Mac OS X and using it to sync data between the two. If you entered your .Mac account information when installing Mac OS X, your operating system is already configured to work with your .Mac account. If, however, you ever need to change your .Mac login information (say, you change your .Mac account), you'll need to follow a similar procedure.

To set up Mac OS X to work with a .Mac account:

1. From the Apple menu, choose System Preferences (**Figure 1.1**).

   System Preferences window opens.

2. *Do one of the following:*
   - ▲ In the Internet & Network section, click the .Mac icon to select it (**Figure 1.2**).
   - ▲ From the View menu, choose .Mac. The .Mac pane opens to the login pane.

3. Click the Account tab to select it.

4. In the .Mac Member Name field, enter your .Mac member name.

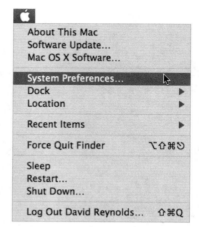

Figure 1.1 To set up Mac OS X to access your .Mac account, you'll need to first open your System Preferences by choosing System Preferences from the Apple menu.

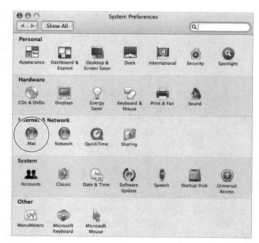

Figure 1.2 The .Mac preferences are nestled in the Internet & Network section of the System Preferences window. Simply click the .Mac globe, and the .Mac preferences pane will load.

Figure 1.3 The main pane of the .Mac preferences lists your .Mac member name and password, and it reminds you of how long you have until your account expires. This page offers more options in Mac OS X 10.4 than it did in earlier versions, including the new Sync area, in which you can choose what information gets synchronized, and the Advanced area, which shows which computers are registered to be synchronized.

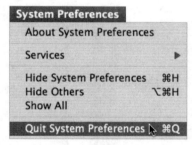

Figure 1.4 Choosing Quit System Preferences from the System Preferences menu will (as you may have guessed) cause the System Preferences application to quit. What you may *not* have guessed is that any changes you make to the .Mac pane are saved automatically when you quit.

5. In the Password field, enter your password (**Figure 1.3**).

6. From the System Preferences menu, choose Quit System Preferences (Command-Q) (**Figure 1.4**).

Mac OS X is now set up to access your .Mac account.

✔ Tips

- You can choose whatever you like for your password, as long as it's 6 to 14 characters long. Make sure it's something you can remember that isn't easy to guess.

- If you don't yet have a .Mac account, click the Sign Up button in the lower right portion of the .Mac preferences pane. This takes you to the .Mac homepage, where you can become a .Mac member by purchasing an annual .Mac subscription.

CONFIGURING MAC OS X

Changing Account Settings

Your .Mac account has a wide range of settings that you can only change online. If you want to make changes to your personal information, credit card information, password, e-mail settings—or if you want to purchase additional iDisk space—you need to first log in to your .Mac account settings using a Web browser.

To log in to your .Mac account:

1. Type www.mac.com in your Web browser. The .Mac Web page opens (**Figure 1.5**).

Figure 1.5 Welcome to .Mac! When you first load the .Mac homepage in a Web browser, you'll be greeted by a page that looks like this. Keep in mind that Web pages can change on a dime, so the page you're looking at on your computer may appear different from the one shown here.

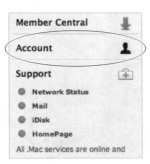

Figure 1.6 In the lower left section of the .Mac homepage you'll see the Account link. Click it to load the login page of your .Mac account settings.

2. In the lower left corner of the .Mac page, click Account to select it (**Figure 1.6**). Your .Mac login page opens.

3. In the Member Name field, type your member name (**Figure 1.7**).

4. In the Password field, type your password. Your .Mac Account Settings page opens, and you can now make changes to your account (**Figure 1.8**).

✔ Tip

■ If you've forgotten your .Mac password, you can click the "Forgot your password?" link on the login page to retrieve it. Simply follow the onscreen instructions.

Figure 1.7 To log in to .Mac, you need to enter your .Mac member name and password, and then click the Enter button.

Figure 1.8 This is your main .Mac Account Settings page. Here you can manage your e-mail accounts, buy more storage, and change your personal information, credit card information, and a plethora of other settings.

To change your personal information:

1. Log in to your .Mac account settings.
   The Account Settings page opens.

2. On the Account Settings page, click the Personal Info button as shown in Figure 1.8.

   Your Personal Info page opens (**Figure 1.9**).

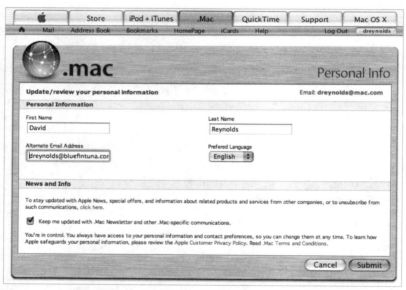

Figure 1.9 Your .Mac Personal Info page lets you change your name, assign an alternate e-mail address, set your preferred language, and request a subscription to the .Mac newsletter. The newsletter is a valuable read, well worth subscribing to.

3. On the Personal Info page, *do any of the following:*

▲ In the First Name field, change your first name.

▲ In the Last Name field, change your last name.

▲ In the Alternate Email Address field, change or edit your alternate e-mail address (where you can be contacted regarding .Mac, in case your .Mac address isn't available for some reason).

▲ In the Preferred Language pop-up menu, select your preferred language in which to view .Mac (currently the only two options are either English or Japanese).

▲ In the News and Info section, click the check box to change your opt-in e-mail setting (when checked, this tells Apple that you wouldn't mind being sent the .Mac newsletter and other .Mac communications).

4. In the lower right corner of the Personal Info page, click the Submit button.

Apple applies the changes you made to your .Mac account's personal information settings.

Subscribing to the .Mac Newsletter

Although it's a good idea to be careful with your e-mail address—after all, one slip-up and you'll be getting more spam than you do now—subscribing to the .Mac newsletter is a pretty good idea.

This newsletter contains special information and offers for .Mac members that can help you take full advantage of your .Mac account. And don't worry about being bombarded by too much e-mail—the frequency of these communiqués wouldn't bury anyone.

CHANGING ACCOUNT SETTINGS

Changing credit card information

.Mac is built around an annual subscription, and therefore it keeps your credit card information on file (just in case you want to sign up for the optional automatic renewal). Of course, as soon as you get that new card with 0 percent interest until 2006 on all balance transfers *and* new purchases, you'll probably want to change the credit card information stored in your .Mac account.

To change your credit card information:

1. Log in to your .Mac account settings. The Account Settings page opens.

2. On the Account Settings page, click the Credit Card Info button as shown in Figure 1.8.

   The Credit Card Info page opens (**Figure 1.10**).

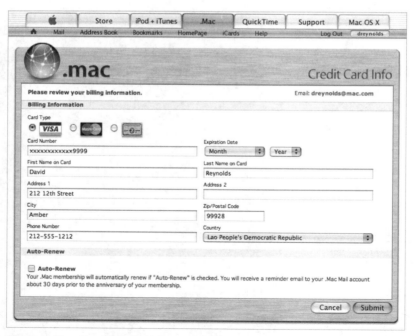

Figure 1.10 Your .Mac Credit Card Info page lets you adjust settings that include your credit card type and number, your name and billing address, and auto-renewal of your account.

3. On the Credit Card Info page, *do any of the following:*

   ▲ Change your credit card number and billing information.

   ▲ Check the Auto-Renew box to set your .Mac membership to automatically renew.

   ▲ If the Auto-Renew check box is already selected and you don't want your .Mac membership to automatically renew, click the check box to *deselect* it.

4. Click Submit.

   Apple applies the changes you made to your .Mac account's credit card settings.

✔ Tip

■ If you do select the Auto-Renew check box, you'll get an e-mail about 30 days before your account is set to automatically renew, notifying you of the impending action.

CHANGING ACCOUNT SETTINGS

Changing password settings

When logged in to your .Mac account settings, you can also change your .Mac password and your .Mac password verification, including your birthday, password question, and password answer.

To change your password settings:

1. Log in to your .Mac Account Settings.

   The Account Settings page opens.

2. On the Account Settings page, click the Password Settings button as shown in Figure 1.8.

   Your Password Settings page opens (**Figure 1.11**).

Figure 1.11. Your .Mac Password Settings page lets you change your password (although you can't view it—all you see is bullets). You can also use it to set password-verification information—namely, your birthday and a password question and answer.

3. On the Password Settings page, *do any of the following:*

   ▲ In the Password field, type a new password.

   ▲ From the Date of Birth pop-up menus, change your birth date.

   ▲ In the Password Question field, type in a new password question.

   ▲ In the Password Answer field, type in a new answer to your password question.

4. Click Submit.

   Apple applies the changes you made to your .Mac account's password settings.

About the Other Settings

The Account Settings page also covers settings that relate to your .Mac e-mail account and your iDisk. These settings let you do the following:

◆ Change e-mail account settings. (For more information, see Chapter 2, "Sending Mail.")

◆ Manage and buy more e-mail accounts. (For more information, see Chapter 2, "Sending Mail.")

◆ Check iDisk usage via a Web browser. (For more information, see Chapter 3, "Using iDisk.")

◆ Buy more online storage. (For more information, see Chapter 3, "Using iDisk.")

CHANGING ACCOUNT SETTINGS

SENDING MAIL

One of the biggest benefits of having a .Mac account is that you get an e-mail address that moves with you, even if you switch ISPs—no more sending out those "my e-mail address has changed" messages, asking everyone to update their address books (which no one does). Plus, if you're like me, you get the cachet of an e-mail address that associates your messages with a computer you love.

Your .Mac e-mail account uses your .Mac login name with @mac.com as your e-mail address. You can use your .Mac e-mail account with just about any e-mail client program out there—provided it can use POP3 or IMAP, and that covers almost any you care to name. In this chapter, I'll show you how to set up your e-mail client to work with your .Mac e-mail account. You'll also learn how to use Apple's Web mail client, which allows you to work with your e-mail using just about any Web browser.

Setting Up Apple Mail

Apple has integrated .Mac e-mail into its own e-mail client, Mail. Since Apple owns both Mail and .Mac, you can expect them to work very well together. (Don't be fooled, though— .Mac plays well with other e-mail clients, too.)

There are three scenarios for setting up Mail to use your .Mac e-mail account:

◆ You haven't opened Mail but have entered your .Mac subscription information in System Preferences

◆ You haven't opened Mail and haven't entered your .Mac subscription information in System Preferences

◆ You have already opened Mail (whether or not you've entered your .Mac subscription information in System Preferences)

✔ Tip

■ Your .Mac e-mail account isn't the only wrench in the toolbox. .Mac also lets you send classy and custom e-mail greeting cards, and it enables you to connect to other .Mac and AOL Instant Messenger users via iChat.

POP vs. IMAP

Most e-mail accounts come in two flavors: the old-school, client-based *POP* (or *POP3*), and the newer, server-based *IMAP*. What's the difference? POP accounts download all of your mail to your computer when you connect, whereas IMAP accounts keep the mail on the server and let you read it from your computer—making it easy to read your e-mail from anywhere but requiring you to stay connected to the Internet whenever you work with your e-mail—even for reading or moving messages. Your .Mac e-mail account can act as either POP or IMAP, depending on which you prefer. So, which should you choose?

One drawback of an IMAP account is that your stored mail counts toward your .Mac storage protocol. Another is that you must be connected to the Internet to organize or sort your mail—even mail you've already read.

You should use IMAP if:

◆ You use several different computers to access your mail.

◆ You have an always-on connection that you can use while you work with your mail.

You should use a POP account if:

◆ You use only one computer to access your e-mail.

◆ You like the idea of keeping your mail on your computer and not on a server.

◆ You work with your mail when you're not connected to the Internet.

SETTING UP APPLE MAIL

If you haven't opened Mail but have entered your .Mac subscription information

This is typically the case if you've just installed a fresh copy of Mac OS X and entered your .Mac information in the setup assistant, but you haven't yet fired up Mail. Typically, folks who already have a .Mac account fall into this category.

If you're using Mac OS X 10.4 and you've entered your .Mac information in System Preferences, Mac OS X automatically creates an account for you in Mail. All you have to do is open the Mail application.

To set up Mail to work with your .Mac e-mail address (Mac OS X 10.3 or earlier):

1. In the Applications folder, double-click the Mail icon to open Mail.

The Mail application opens, and you're asked if you want to import mail from another client (**Figure 2.1**).

2. Click No.

Mail then notes that this version is greatly enhanced and asks if you'd like to take a tour (**Figure 2.2**).

3. Click No.

Mac OS X automatically configures Mail to work with your .Mac e-mail address. You are ready to use Mail to send and receive mail with your .Mac account.

Figure 2.1 When you first launch Mail, it does you the service of asking if you want to import mail from another e-mail client, which is great if you've been using a different client and want to take the leap to Mail. Click Yes to import mail; click No to skip this step and move on.

Figure 2.2 Next, Mail asks if you'd like to see what's new in this version. Click Yes to take a tour; click No to skip this step and move on.

Figure 2.3 This is the first pane in the Mac OS X 10.4 Mail setup assistant. Click Continue to move to the next step.

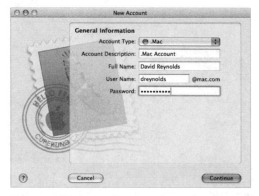

Figure 2.4 This pane asks you to choose your account type, provide an account description and your full name, and provide your e-mail user name and password. Click Continue to move to the next step after you've filled in all the fields.

If you haven't opened Mail and haven't entered your .Mac subscription information

This usually happens if you set up your Mac before you had a .Mac subscription (and thus didn't enter anything in the setup assistant), and you haven't been using Mail as your e-mail client. We'll show you how to do this using the latest version of Mac OS X 10.3 as well as with Mac OS X 10.4.

To set up Mail to work with your .Mac e-mail address (Mac OS X 10.4):

1. In the Applications folder, double-click the Mail icon to open Mail.

   The Mail setup assistant opens (**Figure 2.3**).

2. Click Continue.

   The General Information pane opens (**Figure 2.4**).

3. From the Account Type pop-up menu, choose .Mac.

4. In the Account Description field, give the account a description.

5. In the Full Name field, type your name.

6. In the User Name field, type your .Mac member name.

7. In the Password field, type your .Mac password.

(continues on next page)

SETTING UP APPLE MAIL

8. Click Continue.

Mail checks your connection information to make sure you can connect (**Figure 2.5**). After this check is complete, a summary pane opens (**Figure 2.6**).

9. Click Continue.

The Conclusion pane opens, offering you the choice of importing mailboxes or creating another account (**Figure 2.7**).

10. Click Done to finish.

You're ready to use Mac OS X 10.4 Mail to send and receive e-mail with your .Mac e-mail address.

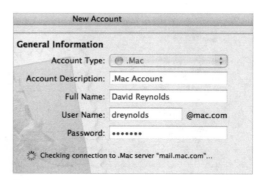

Figure 2.5 After you've clicked Continue, Mail checks the information you've entered to ensure that all of the connections are good.

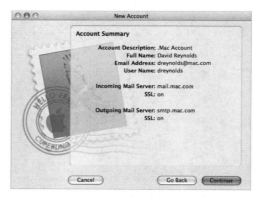

Figure 2.6 Mail presents you with a summary of your new Mail account settings.

Figure 2.7 Finally, when your account is created, you can choose to import mail, create another account, or click the Done button and go on about your business.

Figure 2.8 Creating a new Mail account in Mac OS X 10.3 is fairly simple, and Mail gives you a blank slate from which to start.

Figure 2.9 After you've filled in the pertinent information, you can click OK to create your account.

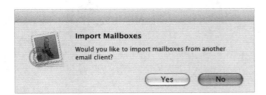

Figure 2.10 Again, Mail asks if you care to bring e-mail messages over from another e-mail program. Click Yes to import mail messages; click No to skip this step.

To set up Mail to work with your .Mac e-mail address (Mac OS X 10.3 or earlier):

1. In the Applications folder, double-click the Mail icon to open Mail.

   The Mail application opens, and you're asked to set up an account (**Figure 2.8**).

2. In the Full Name field, type your name.

3. In the Email Address field, type your .Mac e-mail address, which is your .Mac login plus @mac.com.

4. In the Incoming Mail Server field, type `mail.mac.com`.

5. From the Account Type pop-up menu, choose POP or IMAP.

6. In the User Name field, type your .Mac login.

7. In the Password field, type your .Mac password.

8. In the Outgoing Mail Server (SMTP) field, type `smtp.mac.com`.

9. Click OK (**Figure 2.9**).

   You're asked if you want to import mail from another client (**Figure 2.10**).

(continues on next page)

SETTING UP APPLE MAIL

10. Click No.

You're asked if you want to find out about the new features in Mail (**Figure 2.11**).

11. Click No.

You're ready to use Mail to send and receive e-mail with your .Mac e-mail address.

If you've already opened Mail

If you've opened Mail but haven't entered your .Mac information, you need to manually configure your account. This simply means that you need to provide more information when setting up your account.

To set up Mail to work with your .Mac e-mail address (Mac OS X 10.4):

1. In the Applications folder, double-click the Mail icon to open Mail.

The Mail application opens.

2. From the Mail menu, choose Preferences (**Figure 2.12**).

Mail's Preferences window opens with the Account Information tab selected (**Figure 2.13**).

Figure 2.11 Again, Mail asks if you'd like to see what's new in this version. Click Yes to take a tour; click No to skip this step and move on.

Figure 2.12 To access Mail's preferences, choose Preferences from the Mail menu or press Command-, (comma).

Figure 2.13 Using Mail's Accounts preferences, you can create and manage e-mail accounts in Mail. Here, no e-mail accounts exist yet.

SETTING UP APPLE MAIL

Figure 2.14 Once you've entered your .Mac account information, the Account Summary window shows you how the account has been set up.

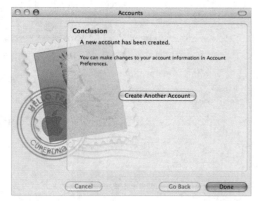

Figure 2.15 After your account has been created, Mail gives you the option of creating another account or simply clicking Done and moving on with your life.

3. In the lower left corner of the window, click the plus (+) button.

   Mail's setup assistant opens to the General Information pane as shown in Figure 2.4.

4. From the Account Type pop-up menu, choose .Mac.

5. In the Account Description field, give the account a description.

6. In the Full Name field, type your name.

7. In the User Name field, type your .Mac member name.

8. In the Password field, type your .Mac password.

9. Click Continue.

   Mail checks your connection information to make sure you can connect. After this check is complete, the Account Summary window opens (**Figure 2.14**).

10. Click Continue.

    The Conclusion window opens, offering you the chance to import mailboxes or create another account (**Figure 2.15**).

11. Click Done.

    You're ready to use Mac OS X 10.4 Mail to send and receive e-mail with your .Mac e-mail address.

To set up Mail to work with your .Mac e-mail address (Mac OS X 10.3):

1. In the Applications folder, double-click the Mail icon to open Mail.

   The Mail application opens.

2. From the Mail menu, choose Preferences as shown in Figure 2.12.

   Mail's Preferences window opens.

3. If it's not already selected, click the Accounts button.

   The Accounts pane opens (**Figure 2.16**).

4. In the lower left corner of the window, click the plus (+) button.

   A new Mail account is created, and the Account Information tab is automatically selected (**Figure 2.17**).

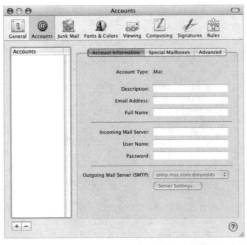

Figure 2.16 Mail's Accounts preferences let you create and manage e-mail accounts in Mail. Here, no e-mail accounts exist yet.

Figure 2.17 After clicking the + button, a new account appears in the column on the left, and the fields on the right are ready to fill in.

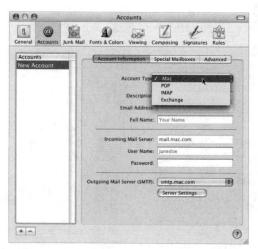

Figure 2.18 Mail supports these four types of e-mail accounts: .Mac, POP, IMAP, and Exchange. For our purposes, select .Mac (and note that .Mac e-mail will also work with POP and IMAP).

Figure 2.19 Once you've finished entering account information, close this window; Mail will now be able to send and receive e-mail using your .Mac account.

5. From the Account Type pop-up menu, choose .Mac (**Figure 2.18**).

6. In the Description field, type a short description of your account (such as your name or your business name—typically a few words).

7. In the Full Name field, type your name.

8. In the User Name field, type your .Mac login.

9. In the Password field, type your .Mac password.

Mail fills in the Email Address, Incoming Mail Server, and Outgoing Mail Server fields for you.

10. Click the red close button in the upper left corner to close the window (**Figure 2.19**).

You're ready to use Mail to send and receive e-mail with your .Mac e-mail address. The account is added to any other e-mail accounts you've already set up in Mail.

Setting Up Other Mail Programs

Setting up another e-mail client to work with your .Mac e-mail account is similar to setting up Mail—mostly, you need to enter a few bits of information in a window much like the one used for Mail. This information consists of your e-mail address, incoming mail server address, outgoing mail server address, user name and password, and any authentication that your servers need.

You can use your .Mac account with any POP or IMAP e-mail client, whether on Windows, Mac OS, or Linux (or pretty much any other operating system that has a POP or IMAP client available). The same method should apply to any e-mail client.

To set up another e-mail client to use your .Mac e-mail account:

1. Open the e-mail client.

2. Create a new account in your e-mail client. Typically, you'll look under a menu titled Preferences, Tools, or Accounts (you may need to consult the e-mail client's help system).

3. Choose IMAP or POP for the account type.

4. In the incoming e-mail server field, enter `mail.mac.com`.

5. In the account ID field, enter your .Mac member ID.

6. In the password field, enter your .Mac password.

7. In the outgoing mail server field, enter `smtp.mac.com`.

8. In the SMTP authentication fields, enter your .Mac member name and password.

9. Check to ensure that SMTP Authentication is turned on for this account.

The account should be ready to send and receive e-mail using your .Mac e-mail account.

Figure 2.20 You'll be seeing a lot of this page. This is the .Mac login page, and you'll use it to enter your .Mac member name and password to access the members' area of the .Mac Web site.

Figure 2.21 The main .Mac Web e-mail interface looks and behaves a lot like an application-based e-mail program. Icons across the top act like buttons in a program, causing actions to happen. E-mail messages are listed below the buttons.

■ If you're using IMAP with your .Mac account, you can manage your mail by logging in to your .Mac account's Web interface. This includes moving and deleting mail, and creating and deleting folders. These changes will show up in your IMAP e-mail client the next time you synchronize your mail.

Using Webmail

Using an e-mail client (such as Mail or Entourage) isn't the only way to access your .Mac e-mail account. Your .Mac account comes with a full featured Web-based e-mail client that lets you send and receive e-mail, organize your e-mail, and even use the addresses stored in Mac OS X's Address Book—and you can do it from anywhere that you have access to a Web browser.

To open .Mac Webmail:

1. Open your Web browser and go to http://webmail.mac.com.
   The .Mac login page loads.

2. In the Member Name field, type your .Mac member name.

3. In the Password field, type your .Mac password (**Figure 2.20**).

4. Click Enter.
   The Web interface for your .Mac e-mail account opens (**Figure 2.21**). This interface looks and behaves a lot like an e-mail client, and if you've ever used a Web interface for other e-mail accounts, you'll probably feel right at home. The interface features a toolbar across the top, a message count and search field, a list of messages, and a message count at the bottom—everything you need to work with your e-mail.

✔ Tips

■ You can also visit www.mac.com, log in to your .Mac account, and then click the Mail button. This will take you to the Web interface for your .Mac e-mail account.

To read a message:

◆ Click the subject line of the message you want to read (**Figure 2.22**).

or

Click the name of the person who sent the message.

The message loads in your Mail window.

✔ Tips

■ When reading a message, you can move to the previous message or next message by using your arrow keys, or you can move back to the list of messages by clicking the Mail button.

■ To sort the messages in a list, click the column header above what you want to sort by (such as date, message size, or subject).

To delete a message:

1. Click the subject line of the message you want to delete.

The message loads in your Mail window.

2. Click the Delete button (**Figure 2.23**).

The message is moved to the Deleted Messages folder and the next message is displayed.

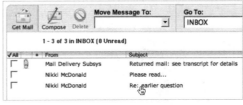

Figure 2.22 Click the subject line of a message to open and read it. Because this is a Web page and not an e-mail program, the message will not be highlighted when it is clicked—but your pointer will change to indicate that it is over something you can click.

Figure 2.23 Click the Delete button to delete the message you're reading.

Emptying the Deleted Messages Folder

When you delete a message, it doesn't actually get deleted. Rather, it gets moved to the Deleted Messages folder, where it awaits its final fate—including a reprieve, if you change your mind. If you *don't* change your mind, you'll need to empty the Deleted Messages folder.

To empty this folder, choose Show All Folders from the Go To pop-up menu. This loads all available mail folders. To the right of the Deleted Messages item, click the Empty Now link to delete all of your messages for good.

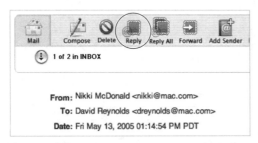

Figure 2.24 Click the Reply button to move to .Mac's reply-composition pane, letting you pen a reply to a message you've received.

Figure 2.25 When you compose a reply to a message, you'll see a few key things—the recipient's e-mail address, the subject line, and your reply text.

Figure 2.26 Click the Send button to send your message.

To reply to a message:

1. Click the subject line of the message to which you want to reply.

   The message loads in the Mail window.

2. Click the Reply button (**Figure 2.24**).

   This takes you to the message-composition page, where you can write your reply in the text field (**Figure 2.25**).

3. Type your reply and click the Send button (**Figure 2.26**).

   Your reply is sent to the person who sent you the original message.

✔ Tips

- You can add a message's sender to your Address Book by first clicking the message in the Mail window and then clicking the Add Sender button in the toolbar. The sender of the message is now added to your .Mac Address Book, and if you use iSync, it will be synchronized with other devices as well.

- To reply to all of the people included on an e-mail message, instead of just the person who sent you the message, click the Reply All button. You can change or add any e-mail addresses—just be sure to separate multiple addresses with a comma and a space (you@mail.com, me@mail.com).

USING WEBMAIL

To forward a message:

1. Click the subject line of the message you want to forward.

   The message loads in your Mail window.

2. Click the Forward button (**Figure 2.27**).

   The message-forwarding pane loads (**Figure 2.28**).

3. In the To field, enter the e-mail address of the person to whom you want to forward the message.

4. Click the Send button.

   The message is forwarded.

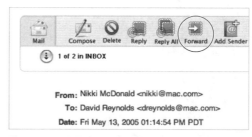

Figure 2.27 Click the Forward button to move to .Mac's forward-composition screen, where you can write a note at the top of a forwarded e-mail.

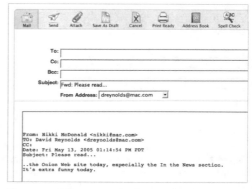

Figure 2.28 When you write the introduction to a forwarded message, the original message's text appears below, including some basic e-mail headers (From, To, and so on).

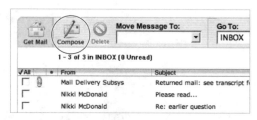

Figure 2.29 To write an e-mail message from scratch, click the Compose button.

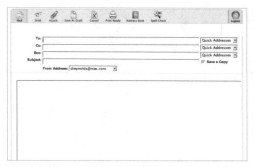

Figure 2.30 Blank screen—not very inspiring. Here, you enter your recipients' e-mail addresses, a subject, and the text of your message.

To compose and send a message:

1. Log in to your .Mac Webmail account. The Web interface for your .Mac e-mail loads.

2. Click the Compose button (**Figure 2.29**). The message-composition form loads (**Figure 2.30**).

3. In the To, Cc, and Bcc fields, enter one or more e-mail addresses.

4. In the Subject field, enter a subject for your message.

5. In the From Address pop-up menu, choose the e-mail address from which you want to send the message (if your .Mac account has more than one address associated with it).

6. In the text field, type the message.

7. In the toolbar at the top of the page, click Send.

   The e-mail message is sent, and you're returned to the main Mail window.

✔ Tips

- If you want to save a message as a draft while you're working on it, click the Save As Draft button on the message-composition page. The message will be saved in your Drafts folder.

- You can check to make sure your e-mail message isn't riddled with misspellings by clicking the Spell Check button before you send. Any misspelled words will be underlined in red, and the number of misspelled words will be shown. Click the Edit link at the bottom to return to the message-composition screen and change the misspelled words.

USING WEBMAIL

To attach a file to a message:

1. Log in to your .Mac Webmail account.

2. Compose a new message to which you want to attach a file.

or

Click an existing message to which you want to attach a file.

The message opens.

3. In the toolbar at the top of the .Mac Webmail page, click the Attach button (**Figure 2.31**).

The file-attachment page loads.

4. Click the Browse button (**Figure 2.32**). The File Upload window opens (**Figure 2.33**).

5. Navigate to the file that you want to attach to your message, and click Open.

The path to the file that you chose appears in the field next to the Browse button (**Figure 2.34**).

Figure 2.31 To attach a file to an outgoing e-mail message, click the Attach button in the toolbar above the composition area.

Figure 2.32 Attaching a file using the file attachment page is an easy three-step process.

Figure 2.33 Click the Browse button to call up the File Upload window, from which you can choose a file to attach to an e-mail message.

Figure 2.34 Once you've selected a file to be attached, its file path shows up in the field to the left of the Browse button.

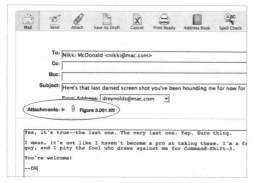

Figure 2.35 Once you've attached a file, it appears in the Attached Files column. You can attach more than one file this way.

Figure 2.36 An attached file appears to the right of the Attachments label, with a nifty paper-clip icon next to it.

6. Click the Attach button.

The file is uploaded to the .Mac e-mail servers, and its name appears in the Attached Files column (**Figure 2.35**).

7. Click Apply.

You're returned to the message-composition pane, and the name of the file you uploaded appears above the message text area (**Figure 2.36**).

8. Click the Send button.

The message and the attached file are sent, and you're returned to the main Mail window.

✔ Tip

■ To remove an attached file, click the Remove button to the right of the file-name in the message-attachment page, or click the disclosure triangle to the right of the Attachments label in the message-composition page as shown in Figure 2.36. Here you can delete attachments and see other information about the files you've uploaded.

Printing a Message

If you're reading a message you simply *must* have in paper form, you can print it in a format that your printer is more likely to appreciate—or at least one that doesn't require so much paper or ink. Open the message that you want to print and click the Print Ready button. A new window will open that contains the e-mail headers and text—with no extraneous graphics. From the File menu, choose Print to call up the Print dialog, where you'll choose Print again.

Using .Mac's online Address Book

One of the best reasons to have a .Mac account is that .Mac is so well integrated with Mac OS X that it makes tedious tasks less, well, tedious. A good example of this is how .Mac Mail uses e-mail addresses stored in your Address Book. After you've set up synchronization and synced your Address Book to your .Mac account (see Chapter 6, "Using Address Book," for instructions on how to do this), you can easily access all of your e-mail addresses from any Internet-enabled computer, anywhere, anytime. And if you use .Mac's Quick Address feature, entering e-mail addresses can be accomplished with a simple point and click.

To use an address from Address Book:

1. Log in to your .Mac Webmail account.

2. In the toolbar at the top of the .Mac Webmail page, click the Compose button. The Compose page loads.

3. In the toolbar at the top of the .Mac Webmail page, click the Address Book button (**Figure 2.37**).

   A page with the addresses in your online Address Book loads (**Figure 2.38**).

4. From the pop-up menu next to each address, choose the addresses you want to use by selecting To, Cc, or Bcc (**Figure 2.39**).

5. Click the Apply button.

   The addresses you selected appear in the appropriate address fields (**Figure 2.40**).

Figure 2.37 Looking for an e-mail address? You can access your Address Book while using .Mac's Webmail by clicking the Address Book button.

Figure 2.38 The addresses in your .Mac Address Book are ready for you to use in your e-mail messages.

Figure 2.39 To include an address in an e-mail message, select To, Cc, or Bcc in the pop-up menu to the right of the address you want to use.

Figure 2.40 The addresses you indicated in the Address Book page appear in the appropriate e-mail address fields.

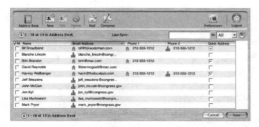

Figure 2.41 To add an address to the Quick Addresses menu, check the box to the right of the address in your online Address Book.

Figure 2.42 Addresses you've selected appear in the Quick Addresses menu, ready and waiting.

Figure 2.43 Once you've chosen an e-mail address from the Quick Addresses menu, it appears in the To, Cc, or Bcc field to its left.

To add an address to the Quick Address menu:

1. Log in to your .Mac Webmail account.

   The Web interface for your .Mac e-mail account opens.

2. In the toolbar at the top of the .Mac Webmail page, click the Address Book button.

   A page with the addresses in your online Address Book loads.

3. Click the check boxes to the right of the addresses that you want to add to the Quick Address menu (**Figure 2.41**).

4. Click Save.

   The addresses are added to the Quick Address menu, available for use when composing an e-mail message.

To use a Quick Address:

1. Log in to your .Mac Webmail account.

2. In the toolbar at the top of the .Mac Webmail page, click the Compose button. The Compose page loads.

3. To the right of the To, Cc, and Bcc fields, click the Quick Addresses menu to select the address you'd like to add to that field (**Figure 2.42**).

   The address is automatically added to the field (**Figure 2.43**).

USING WEBMAIL

Working with folders

You can use your .Mac Webmail interface to organize and sort your mail in folders. When you log in to your .Mac e-mail account through a Web browser, you're presented with your Inbox, which is your main folder. Every account also comes with a few additional folders that may show up—Drafts, Sent Messages, and Deleted Messages—and you can create more if you like. The Drafts folder appears only after you've saved an e-mail as a draft, and the Sent Messages and Deleted Messages folders appear only if you have the Save Sent Message To and Move Deleted Messages To check boxes checked.

To view all folders:

1. Log into your .Mac Webmail account. The Web interface for your .Mac e-mail account opens.

2. From the Go To pop-up menu, choose Show All Folders (**Figure 2.44**).

   or

   In the toolbar at the top of the .Mac Webmail page, click the Show Folders button (**Figure 2.45**).

   A page opens displaying all of your current e-mail folders, along with each folder's name, number of unread messages, total messages, and storage capacity (**Figure 2.46**).

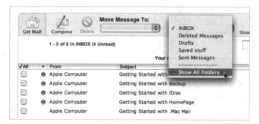

Figure 2.44 From the Go To menu, choose Show All Folders to be taken to a list of your .Mac e-mail folders.

Figure 2.45 You can also click the Show Folders button to see a list of all your .Mac e-mail folders.

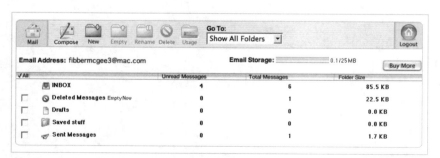

Figure 2.46 The Show All Folders view displays all of the folders associated with your .Mac e-mail account.

Figure 2.47 Clicking the New button creates a new folder in which you can store your e-mail.

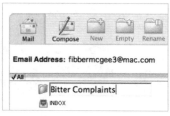

Figure 2.48 You can name your folder something useful or memorable—type it in the text field next to the folder and click Save.

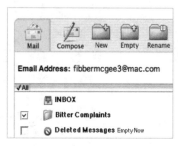

Figure 2.49 To flag a folder for renaming, check the box to the left of its name.

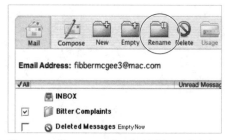

Figure 2.50 To rename checked folders, click the Rename button.

To create a folder:

1. Log in to your .Mac Webmail account.

   The Web interface for your .Mac e-mail account opens.

2. In the toolbar at the top of the .Mac Webmail page, click the Show Folders button as shown in Figure 2.45.

   A page opens displaying all of your current e-mail folders.

3. In the toolbar at the top of the page, click the New button (**Figure 2.47**).

   A new folder appears at the top of your current list of e-mail folders.

4. In the folder-name field, type the name for your new folder (**Figure 2.48**).

5. Click Save.

   Your new folder is added to your existing folder set and appears in your Webmail account, as well as in your e-mail client (provided you're set up to use your .Mac account as an IMAP account).

To rename a folder:

1. Log in to your .Mac Webmail account.

   The Web interface for your .Mac e-mail account opens.

2. In the toolbar at the top of the .Mac Webmail page, click the Show Folders button.

   A page opens displaying all of your current e-mail folders.

3. Check the boxes next to the folders you want to rename (**Figure 2.49**).

4. In the toolbar at the top of the .Mac Webmail page, click the Rename button (**Figure 2.50**).

   The names of all the checked folders are now editable.

(continues on next page)

5. Type in a new name for each checked folder (**Figure 2.51**).

6. Click Save.

Your folders should display their new names.

✔ Tips

■ You can rename any folder except your Inbox folder.

■ You can rename your Drafts and Deleted Messages folders, but resist the urge to do so. If you rename your Drafts folder, you could run into an error the next time you try to save a message. Renaming Deleted Messages seems to work without causing any problems, but it's better to be safe than sorry.

To delete a folder:

1. Log in to your .Mac Webmail account.

The Web interface for your .Mac e-mail account opens.

2. In the toolbar at the top of the .Mac Webmail page, click the Show Folders button.

A page opens displaying all of your current e-mail folders.

3. Check the boxes next to the folders you want to delete (**Figure 2.52**).

4. In the toolbar at the top of the page, click the Delete button (**Figure 2.53**).

A page loads asking if you're sure you want to delete the selected folder or folders. If you've selected multiple items, you're only warned once (**Figure 2.54**).

5. Click Delete.

The folder is deleted.

✔ Tip

■ To select all the check boxes, click the ✔ All column header.

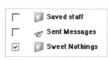

Figure 2.51 Rename your folder.

Figure 2.52 To flag a folder for deleting, check the box to the left of its name.

bermcgee3@mac.com

Figure 2.53 Clicking the Delete button deletes all flagged folders.

Figure 2.54 Before you're allowed to delete a folder, you're asked if you want to follow through. Click Delete to continue.

Figure 2.55 To empty a folder, check the check box to the left of the folder you want to empty.

Figure 2.56 Click the Empty button in the toolbar to delete all of the messages in the folder.

Getting Organized

If you have a ton of mail, it's important to keep it organized—otherwise, you'll be pushing up against that storage limit in no time. Here are a few tips to help you reduce e-mail clutter and stay within your storage limits.

◆ **Delete what you don't need**—sure, the temptation to keep an e-mail may be great, but unless you actually need it, get rid of it.

◆ **Set up a group of folders**—and file messages in them accordingly.

◆ **Trim attachments when possible**—messages with attached files eat up a lot of space, so be sure to download the attachments and delete the messages.

Deleting all messages in a folder

Sometimes you want to delete all of the messages in a folder, but keep the folder itself. Doing so is easy. Here's how.

To delete all messages in a folder:

1. Log in to your .Mac Webmail account.
   The Web interface for your .Mac e-mail account opens.

2. In the toolbar at the top of the .Mac Webmail page, click the Show Folders button as shown in Figure 2.45.
   A page opens displaying all of your current e-mail folders.

3. Check the box next to the folder you want to empty (**Figure 2.55**).

4. In the toolbar at the top of the page, click Empty (**Figure 2.56**).
   The messages will be removed from that folder.

✔ Tip

■ When you click the Empty button, you are not asked if you'd like to proceed, so be sure this is really something you want to do before clicking the button.

Moving messages

The key to keeping an organized e-mail account is to trash the messages you no longer need and file the messages you want to hold on to for a while. Moving messages between folders is easy.

To move an e-mail message:

1. Log in to your .Mac Webmail account.

   The Web interface for your .Mac e-mail account opens.

2. From the Go To pop-up menu, choose the folder that contains the message you want to move (**Figure 2.57**).

   The folder opens, displaying all of its messages in a list.

3. Check the boxes next to the messages you want to move.

4. From the Move Message To pop-up menu, choose a destination folder for your selected messages (**Figure 2.58**).

   The selected messages are moved to the new folder.

Figure 2.57 From the Go To menu, choose the folder that contains the messages you want to move (or to search for); the folder will load on your screen.

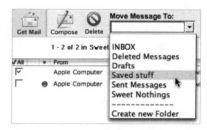

Figure 2.58 From the Move Message To menu, choose a destination folder for your messages.

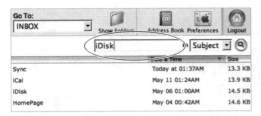

Figure 2.59 Type your search term in the search field.

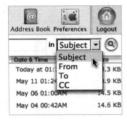

Figure 2.60 To choose what's searched, select Subject, From, To, or CC from the menu.

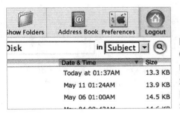

Figure 2.61 Click the magnifying glass icon to perform the search.

Figure 2.62 After you perform a search, the results are shown in a list.

Using search

If you're using your .Mac e-mail account as an IMAP account, you may be storing a lot of messages. Wading through those to find that one special message from the Bulwer-Lytton Fiction Contest, well, it may be daunting when you have 373 messages in your Filed Messages folder, and you can't quite remember the date when the message was sent. That's why your .Mac Web e-mail interface has a built-in search function.

To find a message using search:

1. Log in to your .Mac Webmail account. The Web interface for your .Mac e-mail account opens.

2. From the Go To menu, choose the folder that contains the message you're looking for (Figure 2.57). The folder opens, displaying all of its messages in a list.

3. In the search field in the upper right corner of the page, type the term you want to search for (**Figure 2.59**).

4. From the pop-up menu next to the search field, choose Subject, From, To, or CC (**Figure 2.60**). This setting determines whether the program will search subjects, From addresses, To addresses, or CC addresses.

5. Click the magnifying glass button to the right of the two pop-up menus (**Figure 2.61**). All messages matching the search term load in a new page (**Figure 2.62**).

✔ Tip

■ Search only weeds through one folder at a time. If you have a number of e-mail folders set up, you may have to search each likely folder to find the elusive message.

USING WEBMAIL

Setting .Mac Mail Preferences

Now that you know how to read and manage your .Mac mail using the Webmail interface, it's time to set your .Mac e-mail preferences using a Web browser. By doing so, you ensure that your e-mail account behaves the way you want it to. (Wouldn't it be nice if you could do this in other areas of your life . . .)

Your .Mac e-mail preferences are divided into three realms: Viewing, Composing, and Accounts. To access these preferences, log in to your .Mac e-mail account using a Web browser, and click the Preferences button. The Viewing and Composing preferences only affect how your .Mac account works when you access it using a Web browser—your Accounts preferences affect how it behaves across the board.

Setting Viewing preferences

The Viewing preferences let you set the time zone, the number of messages displayed in a folder at one time, and whether all e-mail headers are displayed.

To set the time zone:

1. Log in to your .Mac Webmail account.
   The Web interface for your .Mac e-mail account opens.

2. At the top of the window, click the Preferences button (**Figure 2.63**).
   The .Mac e-mail preferences load with the Accounts tab selected as the default (**Figure 2.64**).

3. Click the Viewing tab at the top of the page.
   The Viewing preferences load (**Figure 2.65**).

Figure 2.63 The .Mac mail preferences let you control how you see mail, how you write messages, and how your account behaves.

Figure 2.64 Click the Viewing tab at the top of the page to access your Viewing preferences.

Figure 2.65 The .Mac Webmail Viewing preferences let you set your time zone, the number of messages that appear on a given page, and whether all e-mail headers are displayed.

4. From the Time Zone pop-up menu, choose the time zone in which you're working.

5. Click Save.

A message indicating that the change has been saved appears.

To set the number of viewable messages per page:

1. Log in to your .Mac Webmail account and open Viewing preferences.

The Viewing preferences load.

2. From the Messages Per Page pop-up menu, choose the number of messages you'd like to see on a given page.

3. Click Save.

Mail shows only the number of messages per page that you've selected.

✔ Tips

■ Ten or 15 messages per page is usually a manageable number for viewing, unless you go through a lot of e-mail in a day—in which case it might be worth listing more. The more messages you list, the longer the scroll.

■ If you want to show all the e-mail headers when you read a message, check the Show "All Headers" Option box on the right side of this page and click Save. Headers let you see where an e-mail has come from, helping you determine if it's genuine.

SETTING .MAC MAIL PREFERENCES

Setting Composing preferences

The Composing preferences control what happens when you compose and send an e-mail—everything from whether your original message is included in your reply to how your spelling checker behaves.

To include the original message in a reply:

1. Log in to your .Mac Webmail preferences.

   The .Mac e-mail preferences load.

2. Click the Composing tab.

   The Composing preferences load (**Figure 2.66**).

3. In the upper left corner of the page, check the Include Original Message in Reply box (**Figure 2.67**).

4. Click Save.

   When you reply to an e-mail message using a Web browser, the original message is included in the reply, either in the body of the e-mail or as an attachment (if the e-mail is complex HTML) (**Figure 2.68**).

Figure 2.66 The .Mac Webmail Composing preferences let you set what's included in a reply, whether the Bcc header is shown, whether spelling is checked before you send a message, whether a photo or signature is included with a sent message, where sent and deleted messages go, and from whom the message appears to come.

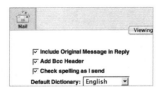

Figure 2.67 Check the top box to have the original message included when you write a reply.

Figure 2.68 When replying to an HTML e-mail message using a Web browser, the reply is included as an attached file, rather than as text within the message-composition text box.

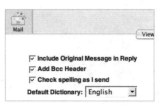

Figure 2.69
Check the Add Bcc Header box to have the Bcc header included in e-mail messages you write.

Figure 2.70 The Bcc header appears in Webmail messages if the proper preference is set, allowing blind-carbon-copy recipients to be added to a message.

Figure 2.71
Check the last box to have your message's spelling checked when you send it.

Figure 2.72
From this menu, you can choose the language in which you'd like your e-mail spell checked.

Figure 2.73 .Mac's built-in spelling checker shows you words that it suspects are misspelled and provides alternatives.

To add the Bcc field to mail headers:

1. On the Composing tab of your .Mac e-mail preferences, check the Add Bcc Header check box (**Figure 2.69**).

2. Click Save.

   The Bcc header appears in all .Mac Webmail messages (**Figure 2.70**).

To have spelling checked before sending:

1. On the Composing tab of your .Mac e-mail preferences, check the "Check spelling as I send" box (**Figure 2.71**).

2. From the Default Dictionary pop-up menu, choose a language (**Figure 2.72**).

3. Click Save.

   Mail checks spelling before you send your message, using the language you've selected for your default dictionary (**Figure 2.73**).

SETTING .MAC MAIL PREFERENCES

To create an automatic signature:

1. On the Composing tab of your .Mac e-mail preferences, check the Signature box (**Figure 2.74**).

2. In the text field below the Signature check box, type the text you'd like to use as your signature (**Figure 2.75**).

3. Click Save.

   Your new signature appears at the bottom of each .Mac Webmail message you send (**Figure 2.76**).

✔ Tip

■ If you're using your .Mac e-mail account for business purposes, include your name, address, phone number, and Website address in your signature to help customers contact you easily.

Figure 2.74 Check the Signature box to have a text signature placed at the bottom of each message you send through the .Mac Webmail interface.

Figure 2.75 Enter the signature you'd like to have appear on e-mails that you send.

Figure 2.76 When composing a message using the signature option, the signature appears in the message-composition area automatically.

Figure 2.77 Check the Photo box to have a photo included with each message you send through the .Mac Webmail interface.

To add an image to your Webmail reply:

1. On the Composing tab of your .Mac Mail preferences, check the Photo box (**Figure 2.77**).

2. Click Choose.

   A page opens where you can choose an image (**Figure 2.78**).

3. Click the Browse button.

   The File Upload window opens (**Figure 2.79**).

4. Navigate to the image you want to use in your signature and click Open.

   The File Upload window closes, returning you to your preferences page.

5. Back on the image-selection page, the path to the image you selected appears in the Step 1 field (**Figure 2.80**). Click the Upload button.

   The image is uploaded to your .Mac account.

(continues on next page)

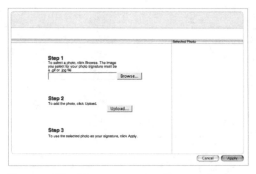

Figure 2.78 On this page, you can choose an image using the Browse button.

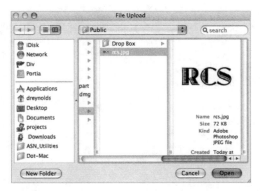

Figure 2.79 In the File Upload window, you can find and select an image to upload.

Figure 2.80 Click the Upload button to upload the selected item to the .Mac servers.

SETTING .MAC MAIL PREFERENCES

6. Click the Apply button.

The preferences window opens with the Composing tab selected.

7. Click Save.

When you send a .Mac Webmail message, the image you selected automatically appears in the upper right corner of your messages (**Figure 2.81**).

✔ Tips

■ To remove a custom image or icon, click the Remove button on the Composing preferences page, and click Save.

■ If you're using your .Mac e-mail for business, you can use the photo feature to add a company logo to your Webmail messages.

■ Check the Save Sent Messages To box to have messages that you send saved. Choose the folder in which you want to have these messages saved from the pop-up menu.

■ Check the Move Deleted Messages To box to have messages that you delete moved to the folder you select in the pop-up menu.

■ To set the name that appears in the From line of the messages you send, type a new one in the field titled From (Your Name).

Figure 2.81 Your image appears in the upper right corner of all .Mac e-mails sent using Webmail.

Setting Accounts preferences

Although you must log in to your .Mac account on the Web to access the Accounts preferences, they affect how your .Mac account works both online and on your desktop. The Accounts preferences enable you to create e-mail aliases, edit existing aliases—which essentially means that you can make them inactive or change the color of the messages that come in to the aliases— forward your mail, set up an auto reply, and set .Mac to check other e-mail accounts you might have.

Aliases, if you've never used them before, are e-mail addresses that don't have accounts associated with them. Mail sent to an alias is redirected to another address—one with an associated account. If your account was me@mac.com, for example, you could create an alias called myalias@mac.com, and all e-mail to myalias@mac.com would be auto- matically delivered to me@mac.com. Why do this? You can give out aliased e-mail addresses without fear—if an alias is abused (with, say, a forklift full of spam), simply delete it and create a new alias. Your original e-mail address remains uncompromised.

Using Accounts preferences, you can also set up your .Mac e-mail account so that all messages that come to it are forwarded to another e-mail account. This is useful if, for example, you won't be checking your .Mac e-mail account, and you want someone else to be able to read the messages while you're away. Simply forward the messages to that person's e-mail address, and every message sent to your .Mac account will be redirected to that person's account.

To create an e-mail alias:

1. Log in to your .Mac Webmail preferences.

   The .Mac e-mail preferences load.

2. Click the Accounts tab.

   The Accounts preferences load (**Figure 2.82**).

3. In the Email Aliases section at the top of the page, click the Add button.

   The New Email Alias page loads (**Figure 2.83**).

4. In the text box, type in an e-mail alias (it can't have any spaces or other non-alphanumeric characters, or it won't work) (**Figure 2.84**).

5. Click the radio button next to the color you'd like to assign to messages sent to that alias (Figure 2.83).

6. Click the Create Alias button.

   The new e-mail alias is now ready. You can send e-mail to that alias (with @mac.com at the end, as in myname54@mac.com), and it will arrive in your main .Mac Inbox.

✔ Tip

- You can have up to five aliases at a time on a given .Mac account. If you have five aliases and you delete one, you'll have to wait seven days before you can create a new alias.

Figure 2.82 The .Mac mail Accounts preferences let you create and manage e-mail aliases, forward e-mail, check other e-mail accounts, and set an automatic reply.

Figure 2.83 The e-mail alias page allows you to create an e-mail alias and choose a color for mail sent to that alias.

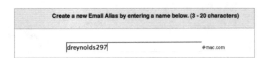

Figure 2.84 Type a word or phrase that you'd like to use for an alias—but remember, you can't use spaces or non-alphanumeric characters.

Figure 2.85 To edit or delete an e-mail alias, click the radio button to the left of the alias, and then click the Edit or Delete button.

Figure 2.86 On the alias-editing page, you can choose a color for an alias or set whether or not an alias is active.

Figure 2.87 Click the radio button next to the e-mail alias you want to delete.

Figure 2.88 Click the Delete button to delete the alias.

To edit an existing alias:

1. On the Accounts tab of your .Mac Webmail preferences, click the radio button next to the alias that you want to edit (**Figure 2.85**).

   The Edit button becomes active.

2. Click the Edit button.

   The alias-editing page loads (**Figure 2.86**).

3. *Do one of the following:*

   ▲ To turn on an alias, click the Active radio button.

   ▲ To turn off an alias, click the Inactive radio button.

   ▲ To change the color of messages arriving at that alias, click the radio button next to your preferred color.

4. Click Save.

   The changes to your alias take effect immediately.

To delete an existing alias:

1. On the Accounts tab of your .Mac Webmail preferences, click the radio button next to the alias that you want to delete (**Figure 2.87**).

   The Delete button becomes active.

2. Click the Delete button.

   A new page opens asking if you're sure you want to delete the alias (**Figure 2.88**).

3. Click Delete.

   The alias is deleted from your account and can no longer be reused.

✔ Tip

■ Remember: Once you delete an e-mail alias, it can't be reused, so be sure this is something you want to do.

To forward all of your .Mac mail:

1. On the Accounts tab of your .Mac Webmail preferences, check the Email Forwarding box (**Figure 2.89**).

2. In the text field below the Email Forwarding check box, type the e-mail address to which you want the messages forwarded.

3. Click Save.

   Your messages are forwarded to the account you specified until you turn off mail forwarding.

✔ Tip

- If you want to leave the forwarded messages in your .Mac e-mail account, be sure to check the Leave Forwarded Messages on Server check box. To retrieve these messages later, simply connect to your .Mac account with your e-mail client and check your mail as you normally would.

To set up an auto reply:

1. On the Accounts tab of your .Mac Webmail preferences, check the Auto Reply box (**Figure 2.90**).

2. In the text box below the Auto Reply check box, type the message that you want to have sent as your auto reply.

3. Click Save.

   Your automatic reply is sent to everyone who sends you an e-mail message.

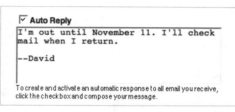

Figure 2.89 Check the Email Forwarding box and provide an e-mail address as the destination for forwarded mail, if you want your .Mac e-mail to arrive in another e-mail inbox.

Figure 2.90 Anyone who sends a message to your .Mac e-mail address will receive the text you type into the Auto Reply text box as a reply.

Setting .Mac Address Book Preferences

You can control how .Mac works with your contact information by setting your .Mac Address Book preferences. These preferences govern how contacts are handled and whether syncing is turned on.

To get to your .Mac Address Book information, log in to your .Mac account and open your Address Book. Click the Preferences button in the toolbar to load the preferences. Here's what all the settings mean:

- **Contacts Per Page**—This setting defaults to displaying 10 contacts per page, but you can set it to 10, 15, 20, 25, 30, or 50. How big is your monitor?

- **Display Order**—Sets how contacts are sorted (by first name, last name or last name, first name).

- **Default Email**—You can choose which e-mail address—Home or Work—is used as the default address when sending messages.

- **Default Phone #1**—Allows you to select which phone is used as default phone number one: Home, Work, Mobile, or Fax.

- **Default Phone #2**— Allows you to select which phone is used as default phone number two: Home, Work, Mobile, or Fax.

- **Default Sort Order**—Lets you choose how contacts are sorted by default: by e-mail address, last name, or first name.

- **Turn On .Mac Address Book Synchronization**—You use this check box to turn on synchronization between your .Mac Address Book and the Address Book on any computer registered with your .Mac account (either via .Mac System Preferences for Mac OS X 10.4 users or via iSync for Mac OS X 10.3 users).

To check other e-mail accounts:

1. On the Accounts tab of your .Mac Webmail preferences, scroll down to the Check Other POP Mail section (**Figure 2.91**).

2. In the Description field, type the e-mail address of the account you want to check.

3. In the Incoming Mail Server field, enter the incoming mail server for the account you want to check (**Figure 2.92**).

4. In the User Name field, enter the member name of the account you want to check (**Figure 2.93**). Typically, the user name is the first part of the e-mail address, before the @ symbol. Check with the service provider that handles that particular e-mail address to be sure.

5. In the Password field, enter the password of the account you want to check. All e-mail accounts have associated passwords (or they should). This is what you typed in when you first set up your e-mail account; if you're not sure what this is, check with the service provider that handles that particular e-mail address.

Figure 2.91 Filling in the relevant fields enables you to check other e-mail accounts and import that mail into your e-mail Inbox.

Figure 2.92 Your incoming mail server address (and a short description of the account) are key to checking another e-mail account.

Figure 2.93 Provide your .Mac member name and password to check e-mail from another account.

☑ **Leave Messages on Server**   Get Other Mail

Figure 2.94 Check this box to ensure that messages are left on the original mail server.

6. Check the Leave Messages on Server box if you want the messages to remain on the other mail server for later pickup (**Figure 2.94**).

7. Click the Get Other Mail button.

   After a short delay, any mail waiting in the other account is imported into the Inbox of the .Mac Webmail interface.

✔ Tips

- Using .Mac Webmail to check mail in another account comes in handy when you don't have access to your e-mail client (or any e-mail client, for that matter). One caveat: The account you're checking must be a POP account—this won't work properly with an IMAP account.

- Once you're done working with your e-mail, you'll want to log out of your .Mac account. To do so, simply click your user name in the Log Out area on the right side of the toolbar or click the Logout button in the Mail toolbar (either of which logs you out of your .Mac account).

SETTING .MAC MAIL PREFERENCES

About iCards

iCards aren't part of your .Mac e-mail account, but they work closely with it. Your .Mac account comes with hundreds of high-quality electronic greeting cards that you can send to anyone via e-mail. There are a number of categories to choose from (just like going into your own Hallmark store), including seasonal cards, birthdays, romance, get well, and several others. If you're feeling extra-creative, you can send a custom iCard—one that contains your own pictures—rather than using one of the pre-fab pictures.

To send an iCard:

1. Go to www.mac.com and log in to your .Mac account.

   The main .Mac page loads.

2. In the toolbar at the top of the page, click the iCards link (**Figure 2.95**).

   The iCards page loads.

3. Click the card you want to send to select it.

   The Compose/Edit page loads (**Figure 2.96**).

4. Click the radio button next to the font you want to use.

Figure 2.95 Click the iCards link in the toolbar to be taken to the main iCards page.

Figure 2.96 On the Compose/Edit page, you can create your own custom iCard.

ABOUT iCARDS

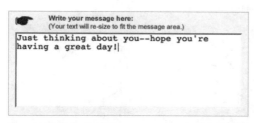

Figure 2.97 Type the message you want to send in the text field.

Figure 2.98 Enter the pertinent address information for your iCard on the Address & Send page.

Figure 2.99 Type the e-mail addresses to which you want to send the card in the e-mail addresses field.

5. In the message text box, type your message (**Figure 2.97**).

6. In the lower right corner of the page, click the Continue button.

The Address & Send page loads with the name and e-mail address associated with your .Mac account already entered in the appropriate fields (**Figure 2.98**).

7. In the "Enter your name" field, type your name if the information that's already entered is incorrect.

8. In the "Enter your email" field, type your e-mail address if the information that's already entered is incorrect (**Figure 2.99**).

(continues on next page)

9. *Do one or more of the following:*

▲ From the Choose a Quick Address pop-up menu, choose the e-mail addresses to which you want to send the card from your Quick Address list.

▲ In the "Enter emails" field, type the e-mail addresses to which you want to send the card. If you want to send the card to more than one email address, separate multiple addresses by commas.

▲ Click the Address Book button to select e-mail addresses from your .Mac Address Book. Check the boxes next to the addresses you want to use, and then click Return to Card (**Figure 2.100**).

10. In the upper right corner of the page, click the Send Card button (**Figure 2.101**).

The card is sent to the e-mail addresses you've specified, and you're given a hearty congratulations on a job well done (**Figure 2.102**).

✔ Tips

■ To view all of the card styles before making your selection, click Browse All Cards at the bottom of the iCards Categories list.

■ To have a copy of the iCard sent to you as well, check the "Send myself a copy" box before sending the card.

■ If you want the people to whom you're sending the card to be unable to see who else received it, check the "Hide distribution list" box.

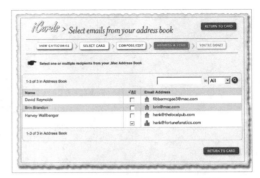

Figure 2.100 Check the boxes for the addresses from your Address Book to which you want to send the iCard.

Figure 2.101 Click the Send Card button to send the iCard.

Figure 2.102 Nice work—you've sent an iCard!

Figure 2.103 The Create Your Own link is your key to making a custom iCard.

Figure 2.104 When you select an image from your iDisk for an iCard, a preview appears on the right.

Figure 2.105 On the Compose/Edit page you can add custom text to your custom card.

To send a custom iCard:

1. Go to www.mac.com and log in to your .Mac account.

   The main .Mac page loads.

2. In the toolbar at the top of the page, click the iCards link.

   The iCards page loads.

3. In the iCards Categories list on the right, click Create Your Own (**Figure 2.103**).

   The Select Image page loads. The column on the left shows the contents of your iDisk's Pictures folder.

4. From the left column, click an image to select it.

   A preview of the image loads on the right (**Figure 2.104**).

5. Click the Select This Image button.

   The Compose/Edit page loads (**Figure 2.105**).

6. Click the radio button next to the font you want to use.

7. In the message text box, type your message.

8. Check the "Resize your image to fit card" box to trim the image to proper size.

9. Click the Continue button.

   The Address & Send page loads with the name and e-mail address associated with your .Mac account already entered in the appropriate fields.

10. In the "Enter your name" field, type your name if the information that's already entered is incorrect.

   (continues on next page)

11. In the "Enter your email" field, type your e-mail address if the information that's already entered is incorrect.

12. *Do one or more of the following:*

▲ From the Choose a Quick Address pop-up menu, choose an e-mail address.

▲ In the "Enter emails" field, type an e-mail address.

▲ Click the Address Book button to select an e-mail address from your .Mac Address Book. Check the boxes next to the addresses you want to use, and then click Return to Card.

13. Click the Send Card button.

The card is sent to the e-mail addresses you've specified.

ABOUT iCARDS

Contributing to the Members Portfolio

Your .Mac account lets you show off your digital photography by contributing to the .Mac Members Portfolio. Here's how you can submit your art for consideration:

1. Save your pictures as JPEG images, and make sure the filenames end with either the .jpg or .jpeg file extension.

2. Make sure that filenames contain only uppercase letters, lowercase letters, numbers, and the underscore character. Other characters won't work.

3. Make sure the pictures are larger than 312 by 416 pixels.

4. Move the pictures you're submitting to the Pictures folder on your iDisk.

5. Log in to your .Mac account, click the iCards link, and then click the Members Portfolio link. Follow the onscreen instructions to submit your artwork, which will then be judged by .Mac officials—not every image gets selected.

USING iDISK

3

Network storage of one kind or another has been around for decades. Back in the day, if you wanted to move files to a file server, your computer had to be connected to the same network as that file server via Ethernet, Token Ring, LocalTalk, or some other network. If your computer wasn't physically connected to that specific network, you couldn't connect. Most often, that meant the computers that were connecting were in a sort of closed arena—able to talk to each other but not able to connect with other sets of computers.

The Internet changed all that by allowing different kinds of computers running different kinds of operating systems to connect to each other around the world—and that includes transferring files to and from file servers. Thanks to the Internet, you can access files stored online from just about anywhere in the world—a boon for business travelers especially.

iDisk is a .Mac utility that lets you store your files on servers maintained by Apple. These servers store files for thousands of .Mac subscribers. When one of those subscribers connects to his or her iDisk using a Mac, the iDisk appears on the Desktop as if it were a network volume on a file server sitting in a closet down the hall. Users can treat the iDisk almost as if it were a hard drive connected directly to their Macs.

In this chapter, I'll cover how to use your iDisk—how to connect to it, how to copy files to it, and how to use the folders stored on it.

Figure 3.1 Your iDisk comes with several folders already on it. Some of these folders are empty, and some contain files (such as software from Apple and files you may have put there through HomePage, Backup, or Sync).

About iDisk

Your .Mac account comes with 250 MB of online storage that you can divide between your iDisk and your .Mac Mail account. When divvying up storage capacity, however, keep in mind that iDisk also provides storage space to a slew of .Mac services, including Backup, iCal, Sync, .Mac Slides Publisher, HomePage, iPhoto, iMovie, and iCards.

In fact, your iDisk comes populated with several folders, some of which already contain files (**Figure 3.1**). You'll find the folder structure familiar—it's similar to the one in Mac OS X's home folder. Here's a look at what each folder is for, and what's in each one (if anything).

◆ **Backup**—This folder is used by the Backup software that comes with your .Mac subscription. If you haven't used Backup, this folder will have a single file that explains the purpose of the folder. If you *have* used Backup, the files you've chosen to back up will be here. The folder is read-only—that is, you can view the files and download them to your hard disk, but you can't upload anything *into* the folder. That's something only Backup can do.

◆ **Documents**—This is a convenient place to hold your various documents if you need to access them online. It's also a good place to back up important documents (although Backup does this very well).

◆ **Library**—This folder may or may not exist for you, depending on whether you've used an application that interfaces with .Mac. This folder isn't really for your use—rather, it's a place where applications that work with .Mac can store their own data. You can browse this folder, but since there's nothing really useful here, it's probably best to just leave well enough alone.

(continues on next page)

◆ **Movies**—You can store movies you want to share in this folder. Movies in this folder are available to HomePage so that you can easily create Web pages with them.

◆ **Music**—You can use the Music folder to store music.

◆ **Pictures**—This folder (as its name implies) is where you store digital photos and other pictures. Pictures in this folder are made available to HomePage for publishing photo galleries, and to iCards for sending custom iCards.

◆ **Public**—The Public folder is meant for sharing files with others. You can put anything in it that you like, and others can download those files at will (depending on how you have your Public folder set up).

◆ **Sites**—The Sites folder is where you store Web pages for others to view when they connect to your .Mac Web site. When you use HomePage on .Mac, it creates HTML files and the folders to hold them here as well.

◆ **Software**—The Software folder is divided into two parts: Apple Software and Members Only. The contents of these folders consist of downloadable bits of software, all for your use, and they don't count toward your iDisk storage limit. The Apple Software folder has software updates and other Apple-made utilities; the Members Only folder contains special downloads for .Mac members, such as games, third-party utilities, and music. You can download from this folder, but you can't upload to it.

Connecting to Your iDisk

If you're using Mac OS X, there are a few different ways of connecting to your iDisk, depending on what version of Mac OS X you're running. If you're using Mac OS 9, you'll need additional software to connect to your iDisk (see the sidebar "When David Met Goliath," later in this chapter). Your iDisk uses a network protocol called WebDAV, which simply means that it uses some of the same kinds of connections you'd use to load a Web page in a browser. Since WebDAV is a cross-platform protocol, you can connect to your iDisk using a Mac running Mac OS X and Mac OS 9, as well as a Windows machine running Windows XP, Windows 2000, or Windows 98.

Mac OS 9 doesn't have WebDAV built in, so it can't by itself connect to an iDisk. Fortunately, there's a handy bit of Mac OS 9 software, called Goliath, that does the trick. Found at DAV & Goliath (www.webdav.org/goliath), this utility makes connecting to your iDisk a breeze.

Windows XP uses an Apple-created utility to connect to an iDisk; you can download it from your .Mac account. The utility is somewhat similar to Goliath, except that it requires more work to install. Windows 2000, however, has built-in support for connecting to WebDAV-based online storage accounts (much like Mac OS X), and it does not need Goliath to do the job.

To connect to iDisk using Mac OS X 10.3 or later:

1. From the Go menu, choose iDisk > My iDisk (Command-Shift-I) (**Figure 3.2**).

   The Connect To iDisk dialog opens, asking for your .Mac member name and password (unless you've already entered that information in System Preferences, in which case your iDisk mounts automatically on your Desktop) (**Figure 3.3**).

2. Enter your .Mac member name and password, and click Connect.

   Your iDisk, which looks like a small globe with your .Mac member name underneath it, mounts on your Desktop, and you can use it like any other volume (**Figure 3.4**). The connection to your iDisk is maintained until you disconnect it or shut down your computer.

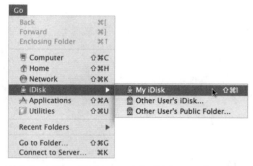

Figure 3.2 Since iDisk access is built into recent versions of Mac OS X, connecting to your iDisk is as easy as choosing Go > iDisk > My iDisk (Command-Shift-I).

Figure 3.3 To connect to your iDisk (if you haven't entered your iDisk information in System Preferences), enter your .Mac member name and password, and click Connect.

Figure 3.4 Once you've connected to your iDisk, you can use it as you would any other network volume. It shows up in the sidebar and on the Desktop, and you can browse it using any view—list, icon, or column.

✔ Tips

- You can also click the iDisk icon in the sidebar of a Finder window to connect to your iDisk, if you've already entered your .Mac information in System Preferences.

- Connecting to an iDisk with a slow or high-latency Internet connection can be very slow. If you're using dial-up or satellite Internet, be sure that no one else (and no other application on your Mac) is using the connection before you connect to your iDisk.

- If you're using a version of Mac OS X earlier than 10.3, you can still connect to your iDisk by choosing Go > iDisk and entering your .Mac member name and password. After you do that, your iDisk will mount on your Desktop.

- Remember—you remain connected to your iDisk until you disconnect or shut down. To disconnect your iDisk, drag its icon to the Trash.

When David Met Goliath

A third-party program called Goliath makes it possible for you to connect to your iDisk using Mac OS 9, which is handy if you haven't yet upgraded to Mac OS X.

To connect to your iDisk using Mac OS 9:

1. Using a Web browser, go to www.webdav.org/goliath and download Goliath (**Figure 3.5**).

    The software downloads to your hard drive in the form of a compressed file. You'll find it wherever your browser normally downloads files (often, that's on the Desktop).

2. Double-click the compressed Goliath file to decompress it using Allume Systems's Stuffit Expander.

    A disk-image file appears on your Desktop, or wherever you normally download files (**Figure 3.6**).

3. Mount the disk image by double-clicking it, and then copy Goliath to your Mac's Applications (Mac OS 9) folder.

4. Double-click the Goliath program icon to run Goliath.

    The New WebDAV Connection dialog opens and asks you to enter some WebDAV information (**Figure 3.7**).

5. Click Cancel—we'll be taking a different approach to connecting.

    The dialog closes.

6. From the File menu, choose Open iDisk Connection (**Figure 3.8**).

    The Open an iDisk Connection dialog opens (**Figure 3.9**).

Figure 3.5 The cutely named homepage for Goliath contains links to Mac OS 9 and Mac OS X versions of the Goliath WebDAV application, as well as some valuable WebDAV information.

Figure 3.6 When you decompress Goliath, a simple disk-image file appears on your Desktop.

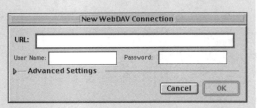

Figure 3.7 You can use this dialog to make a WebDAV connection, but Goliath has a better way to connect to an iDisk.

Figure 3.8 From the File menu, choose Open iDisk Connection to open a connection to your iDisk— using Goliath.

When David Met Goliath *continued*

Figure 3.9 When you request a connection to an iDisk, you'll be asked for your .Mac member name and password.

Figure 3.10 Type your .Mac member name in the User Name field and type your password in the Password field. Click OK.

7. Enter your .Mac member name and password (**Figure 3.10**).

8. Click OK.

Your iDisk opens in a new Goliath window that looks significantly like a Finder window (**Figure 3.11**).

Besides making it possible for Mac OS 9 machines to connect to an iDisk, Goliath is a slick utility developed to allow Mac OS 9 and Mac OS X users to take advantage of WebDAV online storage accounts in a friendly and Mac-like way. It's especially good for the following:

◆ It allows you to connect to other WebDAV-based online storage accounts, so if you have a WebDAV-based account in addition to your iDisk, you can use the same program to access them both.

◆ It works very well with high-latency connections (such as satellite Internet), so if regular iDisk performance in Mac OS X seems sluggish, try using Goliath as an alternative.

Figure 3.11 Once you've made your connection using Goliath, you're presented with an iDisk window that looks almost exactly like a Finder window.

To connect to iDisk using Windows XP:

1. Using a Web browser, go to Apple's Download iDisk Utility page (www.mac.com/1/idiskutility_download.html) and download the iDisk Utility for Windows XP (iDiskUtility_WindowsXP.zip) (**Figure 3.12**).

   The file downloads to your hard drive, but it's compressed, so you'll need to decompress it before you can install it.

2. Unzip the iDisk Utility (**Figure 3.13**).

   The iDisk Utility installer is decompressed, and a folder that contains it appears in the location where you normally download files, ready for installation (**Figure 3.14**).

3. Install iDisk Utility for Windows by double-clicking the iDisk Utility installer icon.

   The welcome pane opens.

4. Read the welcome message and copyright warning, and then click Next (**Figure 3.15**).

   The license agreement opens.

Figure 3.12 The iDisk Utility for Windows is available for download from the .Mac Web site.

Figure 3.13 Once downloaded, the iDisk Utility for Windows appears in its compressed form.

Figure 3.14 The iDisk Utility for Windows, once uncompressed, resides in its own folder.

Figure 3.15 The first step when installing the iDisk Utility for Windows XP is to read the welcome and copyright warning message.

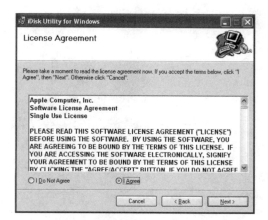

Figure 3.16 To proceed with the installation, read the license agreement and click the I Agree radio button.

5. After reading the license agreement, click the I Agree radio button and then click Next (**Figure 3.16**).

6. If the default installation location is acceptable, click Next (**Figure 3.17**). The Confirm Installation pane opens.

7. To begin the installation, click Next (**Figure 3.18**).

   The Installing iDisk Utility for Windows pane opens, and a progress bar shows the installation of the software. It only takes a short time—under a minute—and you don't have to do anything during the process.

(continues on next page)

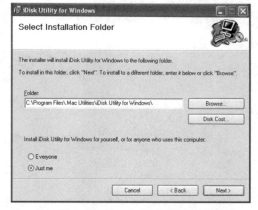

Figure 3.17 When installing the iDisk Utility for Windows, you're given a default installation location and the option to install it for everyone who uses the computer, or just for yourself. The default settings are fine for most people; feel free to change them if you need to.

Figure 3.18 Click Next in the Confirm Installation pane to install the iDisk Utility for Windows XP.

CONNECTING TO YOUR IDISK

8. When the Installation Complete pane appears, click the Close button.

   The iDisk Utility for Windows XP has been installed and is ready to use.

9. From the Start menu, choose All Programs > .Mac Utilities > iDisk Utility for Windows > iDisk Utility for Windows (**Figure 3.19**).

   The iDisk Utility opens, and the iDisk Utility for XP login dialog opens (**Figure 3.20**).

10. In the "iDisk account" field, enter your .Mac member name.

11. In the Password field, enter your .Mac password.

12. Click the iDisk radio button to select it.

13. From the Drive pop-up menu, choose a drive to which your iDisk gets mounted.

14. Click the Mount iDisk button.

    Your iDisk is mounted as a network volume (**Figure 3.21**).

✔ Tips

- Windows may give you a warning stating that it can't identify who created the installer, but this is OK—it's simply a security measure to keep you from installing any bad software, and if you've downloaded the software from Apple's site, you're safe. Follow the installer's instructions.

- The first time you run the utility, Windows will tell you that the iDisk Utility will modify something called the Hosts file—part of Windows that looks up servers across the Internet. This is OK.

Figure 3.19 Choose Start > All Programs > .Mac Utilities > iDisk Utility for Windows > iDisk Utilty for Windows.

Figure 3.20 To connect to an iDisk using the iDisk Utility for Windows XP, you'll need to enter your .Mac member name in the "iDisk account" field, enter your password in the Password field, and choose the drive to which your iDisk gets mounted.

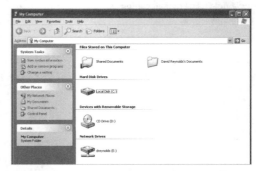

Figure 3.21 Once mounted, your iDisk appears like any other network drive in your My Computer window.

CONNECTING TO YOUR iDISK

Figure 3.22 In Windows 2000, you'll need to open a new window to access the Tools menu. Here, we've chosen to do this from the My Computer window, but it can be done from just about any window, such as the My Documents window.

To connect using Windows 2000:

1. Double-click the My Computer icon.
   The My Computer window opens (**Figure 3.22**).

2. From the Tools menu, choose Map Network Drive (**Figure 3.23**).
   The Map Network Drive dialog opens.

3. At the bottom of the dialog, click "Create a shortcut to a Web folder or FTP site" (**Figure 3.24**).
   The Add Network Place Wizard dialog opens (**Figure 3.25**).

(continues on next page)

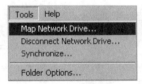

Figure 3.23 From the Tools menu in Windows 2000, choose Map Network Drive to connect to your iDisk.

Figure 3.24 Near the bottom of the Map Network Drive dialog, click "Create a shortcut to a Web folder or FTP site."

Figure 3.25 In the only field in this dialog, type your iDisk URL (which looks like http://idisk.mac.com/ *yourmembername*, replacing *yourmembername* with your .Mac member name).

CONNECTING TO YOUR iDISK

4. In the field labeled "Type the location of the Network Place," type http://idisk. mac.com/yourmembername (replacing yourmembername with your .Mac member name) and click Next (**Figure 3.26**).

The Enter Network Password dialog opens.

5. In the "User name" and Password fields, enter your .Mac member name and password, and click OK (**Figure 3.27**).

The Add Network Place Wizard dialog opens, asking you to name your new Network Place (**Figure 3.28**)—Windows fills this in for you.

Figure 3.26 This is what a properly formed iDisk URL should look like. This one, of course, is the one I use to connect to my iDisk, so it won't work so well for you...

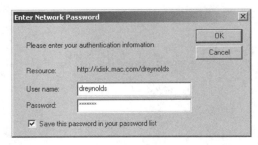

Figure 3.27 To set up the connection to your iDisk, you need to provide your .Mac member name and password in the "User name" and Password fields, respectively.

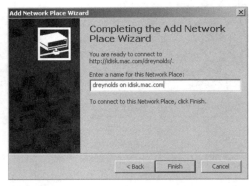

Figure 3.28 The final thing you need to do when creating your iDisk connection is to give it a name. This is the name that will appear under the icon in your My Network Places folder.

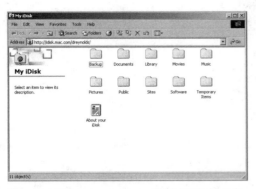

Figure 3.29 When you open your iDisk in Windows, it looks very much like any other storage device, complete with files and folders.

6. If you don't like the Network Place name that Windows provided, type a new name for your Network Place (such as "My iDisk"), and click Finish.

Your iDisk opens in a new window (**Figure 3.29**).

✔ Tips

- You can use the same steps to connect to someone else's iDisk, provided you know his or her member name and password.

- To access your iDisk later, open My Network Places from the Windows desktop, and your saved iDisk location will appear in a new window. Double-click it to open your iDisk.

Using iDisk Utility on a Mac

If you're using a version of Mac OS X that's earlier than Mac OS X 10.3, you should consider downloading and using Apple's iDisk Utility. This gem of a utility lets you password-protect your Public folder and make it accessible to others for uploading. You can also use the utility to see how much space you have left on your iDisk, as well as to open other members' iDisks or Public folders. Although you *can* use the utility if you're running Mac OS X 10.3 or later, there's no real need to, since all of the features are already built into the OS.

To get iDisk Utility, visit Apple's Download iDisk Utility page (www.mac.com/1/idiskutility_download.html).

Moving Files

After you've mounted your iDisk, copying files to it is a breeze. Your iDisk acts like any other disk, so saving files to it and removing files from it is as easy as dragging and dropping. But since you're connected to your iDisk via a network, copying files is likely to be slower than if you were copying them to another hard drive (unless you happen to have a *mighty* fat super-low-latency pipe in your house or at your business).

To copy a file to your iDisk:

1. Mount your iDisk.

   The iDisk is now available for file transfers (**Figure 3.30**).

2. Open a new window, navigate to the files that you want to copy to your iDisk, and select them (**Figure 3.31**).

3. Drag the selected files to the appropriate folder on your iDisk.

   The selected items are successfully copied to your iDisk.

Figure 3.30 Your iDisk, when mounted, looks and works like any other storage device.

Figure 3.31 You can copy files to your iDisk from just about any volume—hard drive, CD, or FireWire hard drive. In this case, we're copying files from a camping-pictures folder on a Mac's hard drive, although the mechanism is the same for any medium.

Figure 3.32 To delete files and folders from your iDisk, first find and select them.

Figure 3.33 To delete a file from your iDisk, drag it to the Trash.

Figure 3.34 You can also select Move to Trash from the Finder's File menu to delete a file.

To remove a file from your iDisk:

1. Mount your iDisk.

   The iDisk is now available for file transfers.

2. Open the folder containing the files that you want to delete from your iDisk, and select them (**Figure 3.32**).

3. *Do one of the following:*

   ▲ Drag the selected files to the Trash (**Figure 3.33**).

   ▲ From the Finder's File menu, select Move to Trash (or press Command-Delete) (**Figure 3.34**).

   A dialog pops up noting that the items will be deleted immediately (**Figure 3.35**).

4. Click OK.

   The files are removed from your iDisk.

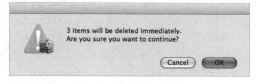

Figure 3.35 A dialog opens, asking if you're sure you want to delete the items. Click OK.

MOVING FILES

Using the Public Folder

Using your iDisk's Public folder, you can share files and folders with just about anyone who has Internet access. This Public folder is a special folder on your iDisk that others can connect to without having to use your login and password. The settings for controlling it are built into Mac OS X.

Using your System Preferences, you can set access to the Public folder to allow people to see and download files from it, but not upload to it, or to both upload and download files from it. Setting your Public folder to only allow people to download items from it, however, protects you from having someone upload objectionable material or fill up the folder with stuff you don't want or need.

You upload files to this folder as you would any folder on your iDisk. The folder is special, however, in that items inside it can easily be downloaded by anyone who has access to your .Mac member name. If you're sensitive about who can access your iDisk's Public folder, you can give it a password so that only those who know the password can access it.

To set access to your Public folder:

1. From the Apple menu, choose System Preferences (**Figure 3.36**).

   The System Preferences window opens.

2. In the Internet & Network section, click the .Mac icon (**Figure 3.37**).

   The .Mac preferences pane opens (**Figure 3.38**).

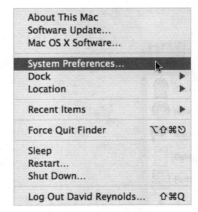

Figure 3.36 From the Apple menu, choose System Preferences to open the—you guessed it—System Preferences application.

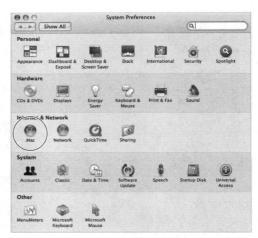

Figure 3.37 Some of your .Mac preferences are built into Mac OS X, and you can click the .Mac icon in the main System Preferences window to access them.

Figure 3.38 The .Mac preferences pane defaults to the Account pane, which contains your .Mac member name and password, and it tells you how long you have until you need to re-subscribe.

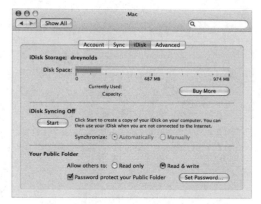

Figure 3.39 The iDisk preferences pane contains good at-a-glance information about your iDisk, including how much storage you have (and have used), whether you have iDisk synchronization turned on, and whether you allow others to upload items to your Public folder (and whether that folder is password protected).

3. Click the iDisk tab.

The iDisk preferences pane opens (**Figure 3.39**).

4. In the Your Public Folder section, *do one of the following:*

▲ To allow users to see and download files from your Public folder but not upload to it, click the Read Only radio button.

▲ To allow users to upload and download files to and from your Public folder, click the "Read & write" radio button.

Your Public folder is ready to be used by others according to the access privileges you've just set.

To password-protect your Public folder:

1. From the Apple menu, choose System Preferences.

   The System Preferences window opens.

2. In the Internet & Network section, click the .Mac icon.

   The .Mac preferences pane opens.

3. Click the iDisk tab.

   The iDisk preferences pane opens.

4. In the Your Public folder section, check the "Password protect your Public Folder" check box (**Figure 3.40**).

   A sheet slides down, asking for password information (**Figure 3.41**).

5. In the Password field, type the password you want to use for your Public folder.

   The text of the password will not appear, but you will see a bullet for each character you type.

6. In the Confirm field, type the password a second time. This ensures that you spelled the password properly.

7. Click OK.

   Your Public Folder is password-protected and you are returned to the iDisk preferences pane.

✔ Tips

■ Your Public folder password and your .Mac account password cannot be the same. If you need to change your Public folder password, click the Set Password button in the lower right area of the iDisk preferences pane.

■ Don't give others your .Mac password—this is different from your Public folder password.

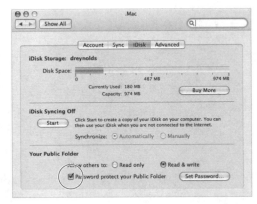

Figure 3.40 Check this box to require guests to enter a password before accessing your Public folder.

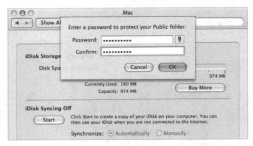

Figure 3.41: When setting a password for your Public folder, you have to type it twice—that's to ensure you have the proper spelling for the password.

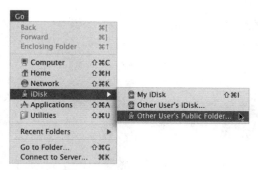

Figure 3.42 To connect to someone else's Public folder, choose Go > iDisk > Other User's Public Folder.

Figure 3.43 Enter the member name of the Public folder to which you want to connect in the Connect To iDisk Public Folder dialog.

Figure 3.44 iDisk shows its WebDAV roots when you connect to a password-protected iDisk. Here, enter the password for the Public folder to which you want to connect (the name "public" is already filled in for you).

To connect to someone else's Public folder using Mac OS X 10.3 or later:

1. From the Go menu, choose iDisk > Other User's Public Folder (**Figure 3.42**).

   The Connect To iDisk Public Folder dialog opens.

2. In the "Member name" field, enter the .Mac member name for the Public folder to which you're connecting (**Figure 3.43**).

3. If prompted for a password, enter one (**Figure 3.44**).

   The Public folder is mounted on your Desktop, and you can upload and download files to and from it.

Connecting to Someone Else's Public Folder Using Mac OS X 10.2 or Earlier

If you're running an older version of Mac OS X, you can still connect to someone else's iDisk—you'll just have to download and install an Apple-supplied utility to do it.

To connect to a Public folder using Mac OS X 10.2 or earlier, go to Apple's Download iDisk Utility page (www.mac.com/1/idiskutility_download.html) and download the iDisk Utility. After the download is complete, mount the iDisk Utility disk image by double-clicking it, and then run the installer that you find there.

Once the iDisk Utility is installed, run it, and when it opens, click the Open Public Folder button. Enter the member name for the iDisk that you want to connect to, and click Open. The Public folder for the .Mac member you indicated mounts on your Desktop, and you can upload and download files to and from it.

Connecting to Someone Else's Public Folder Using Mac OS 9

Remember Goliath, the little utility that could? Mixed-up metaphors aside, you can also use Goliath to connect to someone else's Public folder when you're running Mac OS 9.

Simply run Goliath by double-clicking its icon and typing `http://idisk.mac.com/membername-Public`, replacing `membername` with the member name for the Public folder to which you're connecting. If a password has been set for the Public folder, type `public` in the User Name field, and the password that was set for the Public folder in the Password field (**Figure 3.45**).

The Public folder opens in a new Goliath window, and you can upload and download files to and from it.

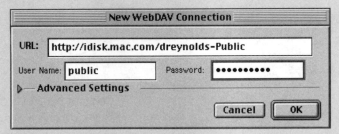

Figure 3.45 By entering the proper information in Goliath, you can connect to another .Mac member's Public folder.

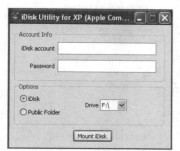

Figure 3.46
The iDisk Utility for Windows XP lets you connect to Public folders as well as iDisks.

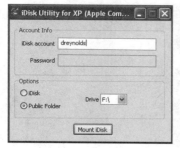

Figure 3.47
Click the Public Folder radio button, and in the "iDisk account" field, type in the .Mac member name for the Public folder to which you want to connect.

Figure 3.48 The "Public login" dialog opens if the Public folder has a password.

To connect to someone else's Public folder using Windows XP:

1. Download and install iDisk Utility for Windows as described in steps 1–10 in "To connect to iDisk using Windows XP," earlier in this chapter.

   The iDisk Utility for XP dialog opens (**Figure 3.46**).

2. Click the Public Folder radio button.

3. In the "iDisk account" field, enter the member name for the Public folder you want to use (**Figure 3.47**).

   If the Public folder has a password, a dialog opens asking you to enter it (**Figure 3.48**). (If it doesn't, the iDisk mounts, and a message appears, letting you know that the iDisk has been mounted successfully.)

USING THE PUBLIC FOLDER

To connect to someone else's Public folder using Windows 2000:

1. Double-click the My Computer icon.
   The My Computer window opens.

2. From the Tools menu, choose Map Network Drive (**Figure 3.49**).
   The Map Network Drive dialog opens.

3. At the bottom of the dialog, click "Create a shortcut to a Web folder or FTP site" (**Figure 3.50**).
   The Add Network Place Wizard dialog opens.

4. In the field marked "Type the location of the Network Place," type
   http://idisk.mac.com/membername-Public? (replacing membername with the .Mac member for the Public folder you're accessing) (**Figure 3.51**).

5. Click Next.
   If the Public folder has a password set, the Enter Network Password dialog opens.

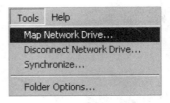

Figure 3.49 To begin creating a connection to a .Mac Public folder in Windows 2000, choose Map Network Drive from the Tools menu.

Figure 3.50 Click "Create a shortcut to a Web folder or FTP site," which will take you to a dialog where you can type in the URL for the Public folder.

Figure 3.51 To connect to a Public folder using Windows 2000, you have to type in the member name for the Public folder, and then follow that with Public? for the complete location. An example for my Public folder is shown here.

Figure 3.52 Once you've entered a location for the Public folder, you'll be asked for the password—if one was set.

Figure 3.53 When completing the Public folder setup, you'll be asked for a name for the connection. A suggested name is already entered for you—often, that's descriptive enough for most purposes and you can just click Finish.

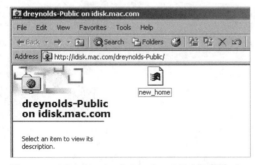

Figure 3.54 Once you've finished your Public folder's connection setup, a new window opens for it, showing you its contents.

6. In the "User name" field, enter public (**Figure 3.52**).

7. In the Password field, enter the password for that Public folder.

8. Click OK.

   The Add Network Place Wizard opens, asking you to name your new Network Place.

9. In the Network Place name field, type a name for your Network Place (such as *Bill's Public Folder*) (**Figure 3.53**).

10. Click Finish.

    iDisk opens in a new window (**Figure 3.54**).

✔ Tips

- Having trouble connecting? Make sure the Public folder that you're connecting to has its permissions set properly, or you (or others) may not be able to connect— or will not be able to upload files, at least.

- A Network Place is a Windows term for a network bookmark—a quick way of connecting to a network service, such as an often-used file server.

USING THE PUBLIC FOLDER

Viewing Other Public Folders

In addition to poking through your friend's Public folder from the comfort of your own computer, you can also access files in his or her Movies, Music, Pictures, and Sites folders using a garden-variety Web browser.

Before you get too excited, it's not like you can just fire up Safari, open up your friend's Music folder, and start browsing her iTunes collection—you have to know exactly what you're looking for. If you know the name of the file you want to access, for example, you can type its URL into your browser and load that file.

In general, the format of the URL is

http://homepage.mac.com/*yourmembername*/*.foldername*/*filename*

Here's how it breaks down:

◆ The first part of the URL is http://homepage.mac.com/*yourmembername*; replace *yourmembername* with your .Mac member name.

◆ The next part, *.foldername*, stands for Movies, Music, or Pictures. So, if you want to access something in your Music folder, type `.Music` instead of `.foldername`. Notice the . before the folder name? This is just a Unix way of hiding folders, and adding a . before the folder name is just how you have to address them.

◆ The final part of the URL is *filename*—this is the name of the file, along with its extension. Replace *filename* with the name of your file.

So, accessing a picture in your Pictures folder might look like this:

http://homepage.mac.com/dreynolds/.Pictures/P1010001.JPG

Or, at least it does for me. You'll need to replace the user name and filename with something that fits your account and the contents of your iDisk.

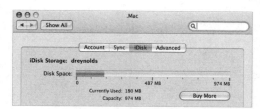

Figure 3.55 The iDisk preferences pane is a handy way to see at a glance how much storage you've used.

About Storage Capacity

Through a built-in control panel, Mac OS X provides an at-a-glance measure of how much space you've used on your iDisk—and how much is available for you to store movies, pictures, Web pages, and other files.

Your .Mac account comes with 250 MB of online storage space, and both your iDisk and .Mac Mail count toward that 250 MB limit. By default, this storage is divided between your iDisk and your e-mail account at 125 MB each, but you have control over how that space is allocated. If you find that either your iDisk or your e-mail account needs more space, you are free to change their storage allotments.

If you're running up against the 250 MB limit, and both your iDisk and e-mail accounts are full, you have two choices: reduce the amount of data you have stored on your .Mac account, or buy more space. While conservation is laudable (even storage-space conservation), sometimes the only thing for cramped quarters is to get a bigger place. You can increase your .Mac storage space to 1 GB for $49.95 per year.

To check iDisk usage:

1. From the Apple menu, choose System Preferences.

   The System Preferences window opens.

2. In the Internet & Network section, click the .Mac icon.

   The .Mac preferences pane opens.

3. Click the iDisk tab.

   The iDisk preferences pane opens. At the top, it displays a gauge that indicates how much iDisk space you've used and how much you have available (**Figure 3.55**). It also attaches numbers to these figures in the form of megabytes currently used and total capacity of your iDisk.

✔ Tip

- You can quickly get to the Web page to buy more iDisk storage space by clicking the Buy More button.

To reallocate .Mac storage:

1. Go to www.mac.com and log in to your .Mac account (**Figure 3.56**).

2. In the lower left corner of the page, click the Account link (**Figure 3.57**).

   The Account Settings page opens (**Figure 3.58**).

3. In the lower right corner, click the Storage Settings button.

   The Storage Settings page opens.

4. From the Manage Your Storage pop-up menu, choose a ratio for dividing your storage between Email and iDisk (**Figure 3.59**).

   The divisions are in 10 MB increments (5 MB for e-mail and 5 MB for iDisk—more for one, less for the other).

5. Click Save.

   Your e-mail and iDisk storage allotments automatically reflect the adjusted settings.

✔ Tips

- The Storage Settings page shows you at a glance how much mail and iDisk storage are being used.

- The e-mail allocation can never be smaller than 15 MB, and the iDisk allocation can never be smaller than 55 MB.

Figure 3.56 To make changes to your iDisk allocation, you first need to log in to .Mac using a Web browser. Type your .Mac member name and password in the respective fields.

Figure 3.57 Click the Account link to access your .Mac Account Settings page.

Figure 3.58 Your main .Mac Account Settings page contains entry points to let you change personal information, credit card information, and password settings, and to manage accounts. You can also change the allocation of iDisk storage.

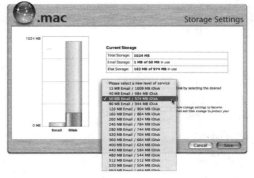

Figure 3.59 You can choose new allocation amounts by selecting from the "Please select a new level of service" pop-up menu.

How to Choose Allocation Amounts

Your .Mac account comes with 250 MB of space, which you can divide between your iDisk and your e-mail account. How should you divvy up this space?

It really depends on how you use your e-mail.

If you use POP as your e-mail protocol, you probably don't need a lot of storage space for e-mail, so you can set it for 15 MB or so, and see how that works. Remember, with POP, when you connect to your e-mail account, you download all of your mail to your computer, freeing up that space.

If you use IMAP as your e-mail protocol, you should start with something beefier, depending on how much mail you intend to store. Try dividing it at 125 MB for e-mail and 125 MB for iDisk, and if you're bumping up against the limit in your e-mail, give it more space. If, after a month or so, you find that you're not using all of that space, you can reduce your allocation.

In the end, it's not critical how you divvy up this space—after all, if you run out of e-mail space or iDisk space, you can always reallocate how the space is used. And if you're really needing to stretch out, you can always purchase a full gig of storage for $49.95 per year.

Buying More iDisk Storage

So, you've outgrown the relatively generous 250 MB of online storage provided with a standard .Mac account? To add some digital room to your iDisk, you can open the .Mac pane of System Preferences, click the iDisk tab, and then click the Buy More button.

This opens your Web browser, taking you through a three-step upgrade process in which you indicate that you want to buy more iDisk space, provide payment (the system remembers the credit card you used to subscribe to .Mac), and confirm your purchase.

Your new iDisk space should be available within a few minutes of making the purchase.

Keeping Your Storage Svelte

If you're like most people, you have a lot of junk on your hard drive that you'd never miss if it were to disappear. The same probably goes for your iDisk. While 250 MB is a respectable amount, you can eat that up pretty quickly with movies, music, and pictures—especially if your e-mail account is IMAP-based. Here are some tips for reducing your online storage usage:

- **Reduce your mail**—If you're using IMAP, you can save on storage space by getting rid of unwanted messages, especially those with attachments.

- **Compress iDisk files**—Use a compression utility to compress files on your iDisk. Mac OS X comes with the Zip archive ability, which is accessible by Control-clicking a file and selecting Create Archive from the contextual menu that pops up.

Creating a Local iDisk Copy

You can set your Mac OS X preferences to set up a local copy of your iDisk. This local iDisk lets you browse the contents of your iDisk very quickly, and it's there even if your network is not (such as when you're traveling with your PowerBook). A local copy of your iDisk takes up space on your hard drive (roughly the same amount as the size of your iDisk), but in these days of 40-plus-gigabyte hard drives on the low end of standard equipment, you won't even miss the paltry megabytes that a full iDisk copy would take.

If you keep a local copy of your iDisk on your hard drive, you can synchronize it with your "real" iDisk via your Internet connection. To do this, you'll choose from two options: automatic and manual.

To set up your local iDisk in Mac OS X 10.4:

1. From the Apple menu, choose System Preferences.

   Your System Preferences window opens.

2. In the Internet & Network section, click the .Mac icon.

   The .Mac preferences pane opens.

3. Click the iDisk tab.

   The iDisk preferences pane opens.

4. In the iDisk Syncing section, click Start (**Figure 3.60**).

   A local copy of your iDisk is created on your desktop, and Mac OS X attempts to synchronize the local copy with your online copy by copying files from the remote iDisk to the local iDisk (**Figure 3.61**).

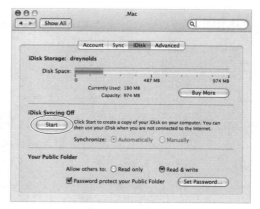

Figure 3.60 Click Start to turn on iDisk synchronization. This creates a local copy of your iDisk, which you can work with even when you're not connected to the Internet.

Figure 3.61 The local copy of your iDisk sits on your Desktop, just like other volumes.

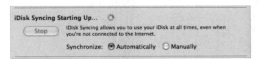

Figure 3.62 When setting up a local copy of your iDisk, you'll need to choose whether or not your iDisk is synchronized automatically.

5. *Do one of the following* (**Figure 3.62**):
   - ▲ To set Mac OS X to periodically synchronize your iDisk copy—uploading files you've added, deleting ones you've trashed, or moving ones that you've moved—click the Synchronize: Automatically radio button.
   - ▲ To set Mac OS X so that it will synchronize your iDisk copy—uploading files you've added, deleting ones you've trashed, or moving ones that you've moved—only when you tell it to do so, click the Synchronize: Manually radio button.

6. Click the red close window box to close the System Preferences application.

   Your synchronization process is complete, and your local iDisk copy is ready for use. When the disk is synchronized, the copied items will be uploaded to your Web-based iDisk. Same goes for deleting or moving items—changes are made on your Web-based iDisk when synchronization takes place.

✔ Tips

- To manually synchronize your iDisk, click the circular arrow button to the right of the iDisk icon in any Finder window.

- You can change whether your local iDisk is synchronized automatically or manually at any time by opening the iDisk preferences and clicking the appropriate radio button.

- Setting up a local iDisk in Mac OS X 10.3 is almost the same as setting it up in Mac OS X 10.4, except that instead of starting iDisk Syncing, you simply check a box for "Create a local copy of your iDisk."

CREATING A LOCAL IDISK COPY

USING HOMEPAGE

HomePage is a Web-site tool that lets you create Web pages with the files stored on your iDisk. Using any of the hundreds of templates that come with HomePage, you can whip up a Web site in minutes—without having to know even a lick of HTML.

Your .Mac Web pages are great for sharing pictures, movies, or files with friends and family. They're not so great, however, for running a business. For a business site, you'll probably want features that .Mac doesn't offer, such as forums, shopping carts, and customized domains. If that's the case, you'll need to host your site through a company that specializes in Web hosting.

Most users, however, will find that HomePage makes up for its lack of business features through ease of use and a slew of professional-looking templates. You can use HomePage to create your Web pages—which is perfect if you don't know HTML or just don't have the time to create a custom site—or you can create your site in a different HTML editor and host the pages on your .Mac account. I'll cover both in this chapter.

Creating a Web Page

Can you really create a Web page in a matter of minutes? You betcha. Although the templates and reasons for creating a Web page may vary, the process remains largely the same, no matter what type of page you create. And that's the great thing about your .Mac account—it provides a bunch of templates and does all the dirty work for you; all you need to do is provide the pictures or movies you want to show off, and write some text describing what you're publishing.

It goes something like this: When publishing a page using .Mac and HomePage, you log in to the HomePage section of the .Mac Web site; select a template to use as a starting point for your page; connect the template to pictures, movies, or files on your iDisk; write some text for your page; and publish it.

Don't worry, I'll go over these steps in detail. Publishing a Web page with HomePage isn't a long process—with a little practice, you can put a photo album on the Web in 10 minutes or less.

I'll talk about how to upload files such as pictures and movies for your Web pages, which templates are available, and how to create Web pages using the HomePage tool.

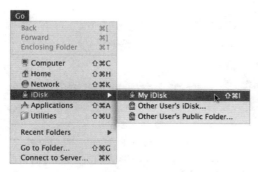

Figure 4.1 From the Go menu, choose My iDisk from the iDisk menu to connect to your iDisk.

Figure 4.2 Enter your .Mac member name and password in the Connect To iDisk dialog, and then click Connect to connect to your iDisk.

Figure 4.3 Once mounted, your iDisk works like any other network volume.

Uploading Files

Although I covered how to copy files to your iDisk in Chapter 3, it's central enough to using HomePage to publish Web pages that we'll cover the basics again here. For complete information on iDisk, including connecting to iDisk and uploading files, see Chapter 3, "Using iDisk."

The reason iDisk is so important when publishing a Web page using .Mac is that HomePage looks to iDisk for the pictures, movies, and other files that it publishes. If it's not on your iDisk, you can't publish it on the Web with HomePage.

To upload a file to your iDisk:

1. From the Go menu, choose iDisk > My iDisk (Command-Shift-I) (**Figure 4.1**).

   The Connect To iDisk dialog opens, asking for your .Mac member name and password (unless you've already entered that information in System Preferences, in which case your iDisk mounts automatically on your Desktop).

2. Enter your .Mac member name and password, and click Connect (**Figure 4.2**).

   Your iDisk mounts on your Desktop, and you can use it like any other volume (**Figure 4.3**). The connection to your iDisk is maintained until you disconnect it or shut down your computer.

   (continues on next page)

3. Open a new window, navigate to the files you want to copy to your iDisk, and select them (**Figure 4.4**).

4. Drag the selected files to the appropriate folder on your iDisk (**Figure 4.5**).

The selected items are successfully copied to your iDisk.

Figure 4.4 Before you copy files to the iDisk, you need to navigate to them.

Figure 4.5 To copy files to your iDisk, drag them to the folder to which you want to copy them.

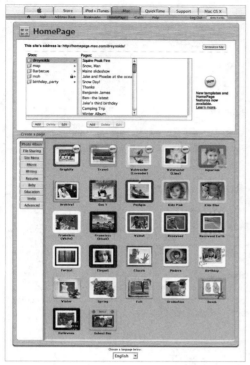

Figure 4.6 When you first load the HomePage section of the .Mac members' Web site, you're presented with its main interface. The top portion lists all of your sites and pages within those sites in a column-style view. The bottom portion shows the templates you can use to quickly create new pages.

Figure 4.7 The extensive Photo Album template set is a quick way to get your digital albums online.

About Templates

HomePage comes with hundreds of templates you can use to build your Web pages. These templates are essentially prebuilt Web pages into which you plug your pictures, movies, and text. Although you *can* publish your own Web pages that you build from scratch on your .Mac site, the .Mac templates do that work for you, so you don't have to know any HTML. All you have to supply is content. The main HomePage interface provides you with the rest, including the kinds of pages you can create, thumbnail images of the various templates, and the sites on your .Mac site (**Figure 4.6**).

The templates are divided into the following ten categories (the categories and templates on .Mac sometimes change, so the ones listed here may not be a complete—or accurate—list):

◆ **Photo Album**—Provides over two dozen templates for sharing pictures that you've uploaded to the Pictures folder on your iDisk (**Figure 4.7**).

(continues on next page)

◆ **File Sharing**—Helps you create an index page so that visitors can easily download files from your Movies, Pictures, Public, Sites, or Music folders (**Figure 4.8**).

◆ **Site Menu**—Sort of the uber-template, the Site Menu template lets you create a menu page that can be used to navigate the rest of your .Mac site (**Figure 4.9**).

◆ **iMovie**—Choose from over a dozen templates that let you showcase movies uploaded to the Movies folder on your iDisk (**Figure 4.10**).

◆ **Writing**—Well, we've already seen templates for sharing pictures, movies, and files, so why not one for text? You get just over a dozen templates to choose from for creating text-based Web pages. These pages don't depend on your iDisk; rather, you write them by filling in some fields in HomePage (**Figure 4.11**).

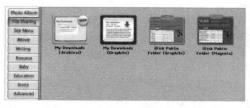

Figure 4.8 The File Sharing template set makes it easy to create a page allowing others to download files from your .Mac Web site (including from inside your Public folder).

Figure 4.9 The Site Menu template set allows you to pull together an index page that points to several other Web pages—either within your .Mac Web site or to external Web pages.

Figure 4.10 The iMovie template set lets you easily put your movies online.

Figure 4.11 The Writing template set provides some attractive starting points for text-based pages, such as newsletters.

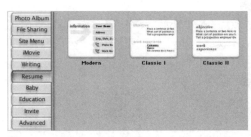

Figure 4.12 The Resume template set makes it easy for you to post your résumé online for others to read.

Figure 4.13 The Baby template set helps you get the word out about that new addition.

Figure 4.14 The Education template set gives those involved in education (such as teachers and coaches) specialized pages.

Figure 4.15 The Invite template set is an easy way to put up an electronic invitation to a party, sporting event, or other gathering.

◆ **Resume**—Looking for a job? Might be worth filling out these templates to tempt potential employers. You essentially fill in the blanks; you won't need to choose files from your iDisk (**Figure 4.12**).

◆ **Baby**—As of this writing, HomePage offers three templates for creating baby announcements: Girl, Boy, and Bath (**Figure 4.13**).

◆ **Education**—Specifically tailored for schools and educators, these templates include setups for school events, sports pages, school news, homework, and more (**Figure 4.14**).

◆ **Invite**—Throwing a party? Choose from templates that include Birthday, Football, and Picnic themes, among others (**Figure 4.15**).

◆ **Advanced**—This template lets you publish HTML files that you've created using an external HTML editor (**Figure 4.16**). Although it's not technically a template (in the sense that you can't plug content into it—you build it yourself from the ground up), it's listed with all the other templates.

Figure 4.16 One lonely template in the Advanced section allows you to integrate any HTML page into your .Mac site.

Creating a Photo Album

The most popular type of .Mac Web page has got to be the photo album. E-mailing digital photos to friends and family members can feel like a pain, especially when you realize how easy it is to simply post your photos to a Web site using one of HomePage's Photo Album templates. Each Photo Album template displays a group of small images that, when clicked, expand to reveal the full-size image. These pages are perfect for sharing digital photos of special events and are nearly mandatory for new parents.

To create a .Mac photo album:

1. Upload the photos you want to use in your photo album to your iDisk's Pictures folder (**Figure 4.17**).

2. Using a Web browser, go to www.mac.com and log in to your .Mac account (**Figure 4.18**).

   The main .Mac members' page loads.

Figure 4.17 The first step in creating a photo album is to upload the pictures you want to put in that album to your iDisk's Pictures folder.

Figure 4.18 Type your .Mac member name and password into the fields on the .Mac login page, and click the Enter button to log in to the .Mac members' section.

Figure 4.19 Click the HomePage link at the top of the page or the link in the left sidebar to load the HomePage tool.

3. Click the HomePage link (**Figure 4.19**).

The main HomePage page loads (**Figure 4.20**). By default, it opens to the Photo Album tab.

4. If the Photo Album tab is not already selected, click it to select it (**Figure 4.21**). The Photo Album templates are displayed.

(continues on next page)

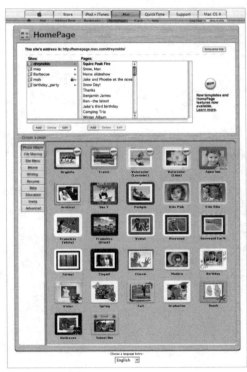

Figure 4.20 The main HomePage page defaults automatically to the Photo Album tab.

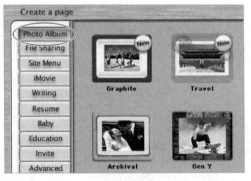

Figure 4.21 If it's not selected for some reason, click the Photo Album tab to load the Photo Album templates.

CREATING A PHOTO ALBUM

5. Click the template you want to use to display your photos from the ones shown to the right of the Photo Album tab.

The "Choose a folder" page loads, displaying the contents of your iDisk's Pictures folder (**Figure 4.22**). Take the name of this page literally. Photos must be saved to a folder within your Pictures folder on your iDisk to be uploaded as a group.

6. Click the folder that has the pictures you want to use in the photo album, and then click Choose.

The "Edit your page" page loads (**Figure 4.23**).

7. Fill in the following fields:
   ▲ In the field at the top of the page, type a name for your Web page, which will serve as the page's link and appear at the top of your central .Mac homepage.
   ▲ In the page title field, type a title for the page itself.
   ▲ In the text edit box below the title box, type a few sentences explaining what your page is about.
   ▲ In the text box below each picture, type a caption.

8. If you want a hit counter, check the Show box to the right of the number 0 at the bottom of the page.

9. If you want to include a "Send me a message" button (which allows viewers to send you an e-mail message), check the Show box to the right of the "Send me a message" button.

Figure 4.22 To choose photos for your photo album, click the folder that contains the photos you want to use in the folder browser window. Once done, click Choose.

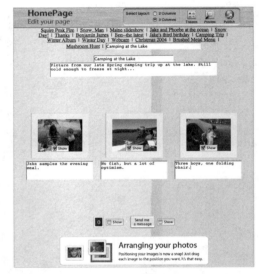

Figure 4.23 In the "Edit your page" page, fill in the fields in the chosen photo album template to complete the page. Here, you'll have to fill in a page title, a page description, and brief descriptions for each picture.

Figure 4.24 Click the 2 Columns radio button to choose the two-column layout for your photo album.

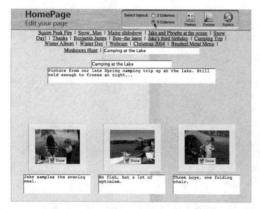

Figure 4.25 Click the 3 Columns radio button to choose the three-column layout for your photo album.

Figure 4.26 To preview your page, click the Edit button and then click the Preview button when the editable version of your page loads.

Figure 4.27 The final step in publishing your site is the Congratulations page, which gives you the URL for your new page as well as the opportunity to send an iCard announcing the page.

10. In the "Select layout" section in the upper right corner of the page, *do one of the following:*
    ▲ Click the 2 Columns radio button to display your photos in a set of two columns on the page (**Figure 4.24**).
    ▲ Click the 3 Columns radio button to display your photos in a set of three columns on the page (**Figure 4.25**).
    The page refreshes to display your new layout.

11. If you want to see what your page will look like before publishing it, *do the following:*
    ▲ Click the Edit button in the upper right corner of the page (**Figure 4.26**).
    ▲ After the page refreshes, displaying the editable version of your page, click the Preview button.
    The page refreshes, displaying a preview of your page.

12. If you did not choose to preview your page, *do one of the following:*
    ▲ If you're satisfied with how things look, click Publish.
    ▲ If you want to make changes to your page, click Edit to go back and make changes before publishing your page.
    After you've clicked the Publish button, you're presented with the site's URL, and the opportunity to send an iCard to friends and family announcing the site (**Figure 4.27**).

✔ Tips

■ To prevent photos from showing up on your Web page, click the Show check box to uncheck them.

■ To arrange the pictures in a different order than the one shown, simply drag them to their new locations.

CREATING A PHOTO ALBUM

105

Create Online Albums with iPhoto

If you use iPhoto to store and organize all of your digital photos, you might just want to skip the Web browser altogether and create your online photo album directly from iPhoto. Select the photos that you'd like to post to your Web page and click the HomePage button at the bottom of the iPhoto window (**Figure 4.28**).

Figure 4.28 Click the HomePage button at the bottom of the iPhoto interface to begin the process of publishing the selected photos to your .Mac account.

In the Publish Homepage window that appears, pick a template, add a title and some introductory text for the page (at the top, below the title), set whether to have the photos displayed in a two- or three-column format, and check the appropriate boxes to include a counter and a Send Me a Message button on your page (**Figure 4.29**). When you're done, click Publish. iPhoto automatically uploads the pictures to the Pictures folder on your iDisk for you. When the photos are finished uploading, iPhoto presents you with a dialog showing the URL of your new photo album. It's really that easy!

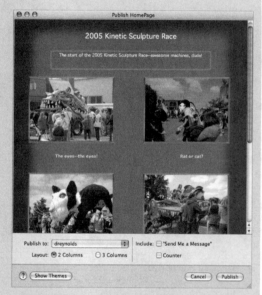

Figure 4.29 The Publish HomePage window in iPhoto lets you set up a Web page before publishing it to your .Mac account. Change the settings you want, and then click Publish to publish the page.

Creating a .Mac Slide Show

.Mac Slides Publisher

P1010055.JPG

Optimizing photo 3 of 3...

Cancel

Figure 4.30 The .Mac Slides Publisher software creates a screen saver of selected photos that others can subscribe to.

Although it's not a Web page per se, you can create a .Mac slide show that others can subscribe to using the .Mac Slides Publisher—a handy adjunct to the Photo Album template. Anyone using Mac OS X 10.2 or later can subscribe to your screen saver, which consists of pictures that you upload.

To do this, download the .Mac Slides Publisher by going to the .Mac Web site and clicking the Member Central button on the left side of the page. Click the .Mac downloads link on the page that loads next. Finally, install the utility and drag a group of photos onto the application's icon. These pictures will be uploaded to your iDisk, where they will be published as a screen saver (**Figure 4.30**). Nifty, huh?

To subscribe to a .Mac screen saver, open your System Preferences, click the Desktop & Screen Saver icon, select the Screen Saver tab, and click the .Mac button in the list to the left. Click Options, and you can enter the member name of the person hosting the slide show to which you want to subscribe. Click OK, and you're set.

Creating a Movie Page

Thanks to broadband (for some of us lucky souls, at least), we can easily view movies online. And thanks to your .Mac account, you can upload your own movies for others to view. Creating a movie page follows the same basic process as creating a photo album.

To create a movie page:

1. Upload the movie you want to share to your iDisk's Movies folder.

2. Using a Web browser, go to www.mac.com and log in to your .Mac account (**Figure 4.31**).

   The main .Mac members' page loads.

3. Click the HomePage link.

   The main HomePage page loads.

4. At the lower left side of the page, click the iMovie tab.

   The iMovie templates load (**Figure 4.32**).

Figure 4.31 Enter your .Mac member name and password in the appropriate fields on the login page.

Figure 4.32 The iMovie templates page lets you choose from a number of templates for your uploaded iMovie.

Figure 4.33 On the "Edit your Page" page, you set up the specifics of your new iMovie page.

Figure 4.34 To complete the iMovie page, give it a name and a brief description of the page, and choose whether to include counter and contact buttons.

Figure 4.35 To have a hit counter included on your Web page, check the Show box to the right of the number 0 at the bottom of the page.

5. Click the template you want to use (my fave is Retro-TV).

The "Edit your page" page loads (**Figure 4.33**).

6. Fill in the following fields (**Figure 4.34**):

▲ In the field at the top of the page, type a name for your Web page, which will serve as the page's link and appear at the top of your central .Mac homepage.

▲ Type a name for your movie.

▲ Type a brief description of what your movie is about.

7. If you want a hit counter, check the Show box to the right of the number 0 at the bottom of the page (**Figure 4.35**).

8. If you want to include a "Send me a message" button (which viewers can use to send you an e-mail message), check the Show box to the right of the "Send me a message" button, as shown in Figure 4.35.

9. Just below the QuickTime icon, click the Choose button as shown in Figure 4.33.

The "Choose a file" page opens (**Figure 4.36**).

(continues on next page)

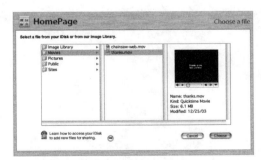

Figure 4.36 Select the movie you want to use on your iMovie page, and then click Choose.

CREATING A MOVIE PAGE

10. Click a movie to select it, then click Choose.

You're returned to the "Edit your page" page.

11. In the upper right corner of the page, click Preview.

The page displaying your movie loads (**Figure 4.37**).

12. If you need to make changes, click Edit in the upper right corner of the page (**Figure 4.38**).

or

If you're satisfied with how it looks, click Publish.

A Congratulations page loads, containing the movie page's URL and giving you the opportunity to send an iCard announcing the new page (**Figure 4.39**).

✔ Tips

■ Although the tab says iMovie, don't worry—you can create your video using a different video editing package and still use it here, as long as QuickTime understands it.

■ You can also select a movie from your Pictures, Public, or Sites folder.

Figure 4.37 After you've selected the movie you want to include on your new page and clicked Preview, the page loads as it would be seen by others.

Figure 4.38 Click the Edit button to make changes to your movie page or click Publish to post it.

Figure 4.39 When you've published your iMovie page, the page's URL is shown, and you're given the opportunity to send an iCard announcing it.

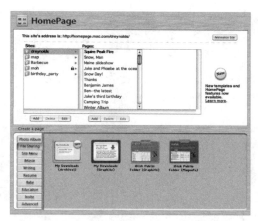

Figure 4.40 To begin creating a file-download page, click the File Sharing template that you want to use.

Creating a File-Download Page

If you want to provide an easy way for people to download files from your iDisk's Public folder, you're in luck: HomePage includes a few file-download templates.

To create a file-download page:

1. Upload the files you want to share to your iDisk's Public folder.

2. Using a Web browser, go to www.mac.com and log in to your .Mac account.

   The main .Mac members' page loads.

3. Click the HomePage link.

   The main HomePage page loads.

4. On the lower left side of the page, click the File Sharing tab.

   The File Sharing templates load (**Figure 4.40**). There are two types of templates here: My Downloads templates and iDisk Public Folder templates. The My Downloads templates allow you to choose any file on your iDisk; the iDisk Public Folder templates only list files in your iDisk's Public folder.

5. Click the File Sharing template that you want to use.

   The "Edit your page" page loads for the selected template. What you do next depends on whether you chose a My Downloads template or an iDisk Public Folder template.

(continues on next page)

6. If you chose a My Downloads template, *do the following* (**Figure 4.41**):

▲ In the field at the top of the page, type a name for your Web page, which will serve as the page's link and appear at the top of your central .Mac homepage.

▲ Type a few sentences that describe your page. This text will appear below the page's title at the top of your Web page.

▲ In the Document Title field, type a title for the file that you're making available as a download.

▲ If you want the file's size to be displayed on the page, check the Show box to the right of the word "Size."

▲ In the description field, write a brief description of the file.

▲ To choose an image for the downloadable file's thumbnail from your iDisk, click the Choose button.

▲ To choose a file to use as a download from your iDisk's Movies, Pictures, Public, Sites, or Music folder, click the "Choose file" button.

7. If you chose an iDisk Public Folder template, *do the following* (**Figure 4.42**):

▲ In the field at the top of the page, type a name for your Web page, which will serve as the page's link and appear at the top of your central .Mac homepage.

▲ In the description field, type a description of the contents of your folder.

8. If you want a hit counter, check the Show box to the right of the number 0 at the bottom of the page.

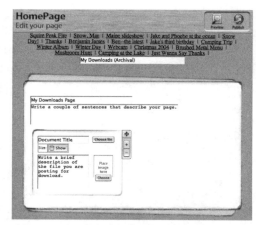

Figure 4.41 If you've chosen a My Downloads template, enter a page title and a brief description, choose an image, and choose a file to be downloaded.

Figure 4.42 If you've chosen an iDisk Public Folder template, enter a page title and a brief description for your page.

Figure 4.43 After you click the Preview button, the page loads as others would see it—giving you the opportunity to make any needed last-minute changes.

Figure 4.44 When you've published your File Sharing page, you're given the page's URL and the opportunity to send an iCard announcing it.

9. If you want to include a "Send me a message" button (which viewers can use to send you an e-mail message), check the Show box to the right of the "Send me a message" button.

10. To see what the page will look like before you publish it, click Preview. A preview of the page loads (**Figure 4.43**).

11. If you need to make changes, click Edit. If you're satisfied with how it looks, click Publish.

    A Congratulations page loads, displaying the download page's URL and giving you the opportunity to send an iCard announcing the new page (**Figure 4.44**).

(continues on next page)

✔ Tips

- If files that you know are in your Public folder aren't appearing in the list, click the Refresh button to see if you can make them appear.

- To make sure that everyone can work with your files—regardless of their operating system—use care when naming your files. Stick to uppercase letters, lowercase letters, numbers, hyphens, and underscore characters only (this means no spaces), and you ought to be fine. And don't delete the filename extensions (such as .jpg or .doc).

- You can specify files from other folders on your iDisk with a My Downloads template, so it's not necessary for you to upload files strictly to the Public folder.

- You can add additional files to the download page by clicking the Plus (+) button to the right of the file-description area—if you're using a My Downloads template. If you have multiple file-description areas on a download page, you can drag them around by the crossed vertical and horizontal arrow tab to rearrange them.

- You can remove a file from the download page—if you're using a My Downloads template—by clicking the minus sign to the right of its description area.

Say It with an iCard

After you create a new .Mac Web page, the first thing you'll want to do is to tell people about it. Thanks to iCards, that's a breeze. When you finish creating a new site, a page opens asking if you want to send an iCard announcement. Click the arrow button in the bottom of the page and you're taken to a special iCard template page, where crafting a quick card with your URL is as easy as filling in the blanks (**Figure 4.45**).

Figure 4.45 To send an iCard announcing your new page, simply choose a template, type a message, and add e-mail addresses to which you'll be sending it. When finished, click Send iCard.

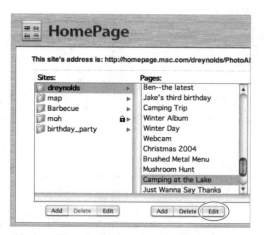

Figure 4.46 To edit a page, select it in the Pages column and then click the Edit button below the Pages column.

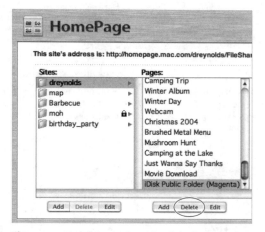

Figure 4.47 To delete a page, select it in the Pages column and then click the Delete button.

Editing Pages

Sometimes, you may need to make changes to a .Mac Web page (spelling being what it is) or perhaps delete a page you no longer need. You can change anything about your Web page—template colors, layout options, captions, you name it—quickly and easily.

To edit an existing page:

1. Log in to your .Mac account using a Web browser, and click the HomePage link.

   The main HomePage page loads.

2. At the top of the page, select the page you want to edit, and click the Edit button (**Figure 4.46**).

   The "Edit your page" page loads, displaying your page in its editable form.

To delete an existing page:

1. Log in to your .Mac account using a Web browser, and click the HomePage link.

   The main HomePage page loads.

2. At the top of the page, select the page you want to delete and click the Delete button (**Figure 4.47**).

   A warning appears, noting that deleting a page is permanent and asking you if you want to continue.

3. Click Yes.

   Your Web page is deleted.

Creating a Site

When you've created a series of Web pages that you'd like to tie together into a logical group, you may be best served by creating a site. This groups a set of pages together for easier access. Your .Mac account not only makes it easy to create a Web page, but it also lets you manage multiple Web sites with the same set of tools.

To create a site:

1. Log in to your .Mac account using a Web browser, and click the HomePage link.

   The main HomePage page loads.

2. On the left side of the page below the Sites column, click the Add button (**Figure 4.48**).

   The "Create a site" page loads.

3. In the Site Name field, type the name for your site.

4. If you want to password protect your site, check the Password On box.

5. If you've checked the Password On box, type the password in your Password field (**Figure 4.49**).

6. Click the Create Site button.

   The main HomePage page loads, with a note at the top indicating the URL of the newly created site. A folder (with the site's name to the right) appears in the Sites column on the left (**Figure 4.50**).

✔ Tips

■ You can't use spaces in your site names.

■ .Mac site names are case sensitive.

■ Don't use your .Mac password for a site's password. If you do, then the people you give the site's address and password to will also have the keys to your .Mac account.

Figure 4.48 To add a new site, click the Add button below the Sites column on the left.

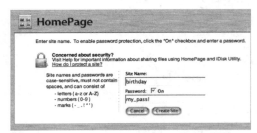

Figure 4.49 Give the site a name in the "Create a site" page. Check the On box to the right of the word Password, and type in a password to password protect the site.

Figure 4.50 Your new site appears as a folder in the leftmost Sites column. Above, a URL for the page is displayed. Of course, no pages are in the site yet—you'll have to add those.

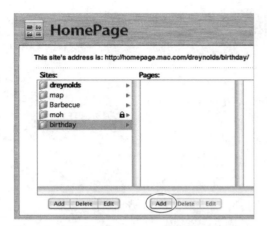

Figure 4.51 To add a new page to a site, first click the site's folder in the Sites column, and then click the Add button below the Pages column.

To add a page to a site:

1. Log in to your .Mac account using a Web browser, and click the HomePage link.

   The main HomePage page loads.

2. In the Sites section, click the folder of the site to which you want to add a new page (Figure 4.50).

3. Just below the Pages section, click the Add button (**Figure 4.51**).

   The "Select a theme" page opens. From here, you can create any type of page you like, as described earlier in this chapter.

✔ Tip

■ You can move a page from one site to another by dragging the page you want to move to the new site folder in the main HomePage interface.

Getting to Your New Web Site

Once you've created a Web site, others can see it at the following:

http://homepage.mac.com/*yourmembername*/

Of course, be sure to replace *yourmembername* with your .Mac member name. This will take folks to your main .Mac homepage. To specify a site within your .Mac Web site, use this URL:

http://homepage.mac.com/*yourmembername*/*sitename*/

In the URL above, replace *yourmembername* with your .Mac member name and *sitename* with the site name that you specify. This takes people to the specified site in *sitename*.

You can always find a site's URL by logging in to the HomePage utility and selecting the site (on the left). The URL will appear at the top of the page in blue (**Figure 4.52**).

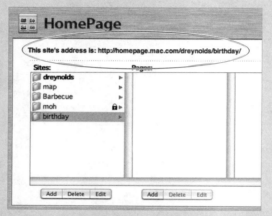

Figure 4.52 To find a site's URL, you can always log in to the HomePage utility and select the site's folder in the Sites column. The URL appears at the top of the page.

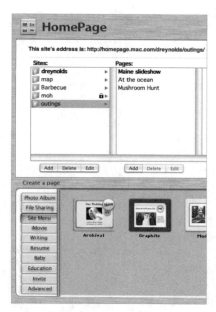

Figure 4.53 The first step in creating a site menu is to select the site in the Sites column and then select the Site Menu tab to load the Site Menu template set.

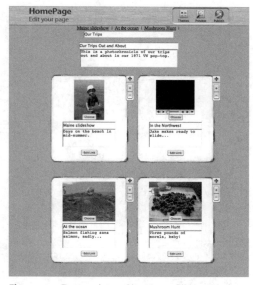

Figure 4.54 To complete a Site Menu, fill in a title for the page, and a title and description for each item on the page.

Creating a Site Menu

Now that you've created all these great Web pages, it's time to organize them with a site menu—and for that, we'll need the Site Menu template. A site menu provides visitors with a high-level overview of the pages in a site that you've created using your .Mac account. The site menu should be one of the last things you do when creating a site—it's the bit that ties together a bunch of disparate pages into a coherent whole.

To create a site menu:

1. Log in to your .Mac account using a Web browser, and click the HomePage link.
   The main HomePage page loads.

2. In the left column, at the top of the page, select the site for which you want to create a site menu, and then click the Site Menu tab (**Figure 4.53**).
   The Site Menu templates load.

3. Click a Site Menu template.
   The "Edit your page" page loads for that selected template. This page shows all of the site's individual Web pages.

4. Fill in all of the text fields, writing a title and description for the page, and a title and description for each item (**Figure 4.54**).

   (continues on next page)

5. To choose a different picture to represent a specific photo album on the site menu, click Choose and select a new picture in the "Choose a file" page (**Figure 4.55**).

6. To remove a page from the site menu you are creating, click the Minus button next to each page you want removed from the site menu (**Figure 4.56**).

The page reloads sans the items you clicked.

7. To add a new page (or external link) to the site menu you are creating, click the Plus button next to the item you want to have appear *before* the new page or link (**Figure 4.57**).

The page reloads *with* a new item. See the sidebar "Adding Links to Your Site Menu" for details on how to do this.

Figure 4.55 Click the picture you want to use as the representative graphic for the site menu item, and then click Choose to set the image.

Figure 4.56 To remove an item from a site menu page, click the Minus button in its upper right corner.

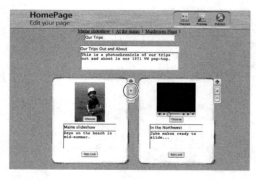

Figure 4.57 To add a new item linking to another page (or to an e-mail address), click the Plus button in the upper right corner of the item you want to have appear *before* the new item.

8. To reposition an item on the site menu page, drag the crossed-arrows icon to the right of the item to move it (**Figure 4.58**).

9. To preview your site menu before publishing it, click the Preview button in the upper right corner of the page.

10. If you're satisfied, click the Publish button at the top of the page.

Your site menu page is published, and the Congratulations page loads with the URL to your new page.

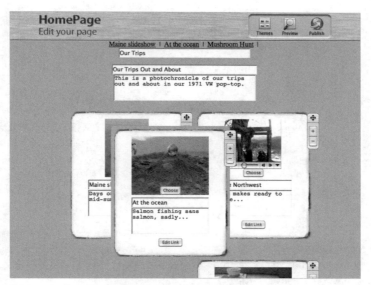

Figure 4.58 Repositioning items on a site menu page is as easy as dragging the upper right corner of the item until the item is where you want it to be—place it between two items to have the moved item appear between them.

Adding Links to Your Site Menu

Remember that Plus (+) button next to each item on the Site Menu template (**Figure 4.59**)? That button lets you link to the following items from your site menu:

◆ Another page from your .Mac account

◆ An external Web page

◆ An e-mail address

To create a section that links to any of these items from your site menu, click the Plus button next to the Web page to which you want to add the link. Don't worry, you won't remove the existing page—the section for adding the link appears below it. Customize this one as you would any other section within a site menu page by typing a title and description and choosing a graphic element (**Figure 4.60**).

To create the new link, click the Edit Link button. The "Edit your links" page opens. Select from the My Pages, Other Pages, and Email tabs (**Figure 4.61**). Here's what each one does:

◆ **My Pages**—This tab lets you link only to pages that you've created through your .Mac account. On the My Pages tab, select a page to link to it from the site menu and click Apply.

◆ **Other Pages**—This tab lets you link to pages other than the ones you've created yourself through your .Mac account. On the Other Pages tab, type in the URL of the page you want to link to from the site menu in the field, and click Apply.

◆ **Email**—This tab lets you link an item on your Web page to an e-mail address. On the Email tab, type the e-mail address that you'd like to link to in the field, and click Apply.

Figure 4.59 Each item on a site menu page has a Plus button to the right near the top—part of a cluster of three buttons. Clicking the Plus button allows you to add a new item to your site menu page *after* the item on which the Plus button was pushed.

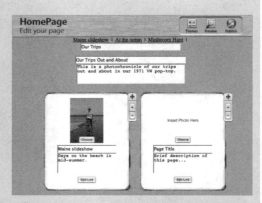

Figure 4.60 A new item on a site menu page is mostly blank—it's up to you to select a graphic and type in a page title and description.

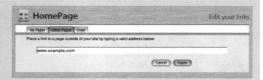

Figure 4.61 By clicking the Edit Link button on an item in a site menu, you can link to another .Mac element, a Web page outside of .Mac, or an e-mail address.

Figure 4.62 To edit a site, click its name in the Sites column, and then click the Edit button below the Sites column.

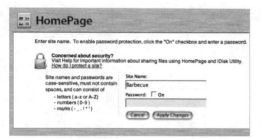

Figure 4.63 When the "Edit your site" page loads, you can change the site's name and either assign or remove a password.

✔ Tip

- To reorder the pages within a site, drag them up or down in the list on the main HomePage page. The page at the top of a given site is the one that loads first when the site is visited—it becomes the index for that site.

Editing Sites

Web sites are not set in stone. After you've created your site, you're likely to want to go back and make occasional changes. Although you'll make most of your changes to individual pages, which we've already covered in this chapter, you can make a few sitewide changes, should the need arise. You can change the name of the site, change the password, or delete the site altogether.

To edit a site:

1. Log in to your .Mac account using a Web browser, and click the HomePage button. The main HomePage page loads.

2. In the Sites column, select the site that you want to edit (**Figure 4.62**).

3. At the bottom of the Sites column, click the Edit button. The "Edit your site" page loads.

4. *Do one or all of the following* (**Figure 4.63**):
   ▲ In the Site Name field, type in a new name for your site.
   ▲ If you'd like to set a password for the site, check the Password On box, if it isn't already checked, and type a password in the field below it.
   ▲ If you'd like to remove password protection from your site, click the Password On box to deselect it.
   ▲ If you'd like to change the password for your site, type in a new password.

5. Click Apply Changes. Your new site settings are applied automatically.

To delete a site:

1. Log in to your .Mac account using a Web browser, and click the HomePage button.

   The main HomePage page loads.

2. In the Sites column, select the site that you want to delete.

3. Click the Delete button.

   The "Delete your site" page loads, asking if you're sure you want to delete the site.

4. Click Yes.

   Your site is automatically deleted.

Advanced Web Publishing

Although your .Mac account isn't a full-service professional-level Web hosting account, it *is* capable of doing more than publishing photo albums and file-download pages. In fact, as long as your Web pages don't rely on fancy services such as CGIs, PHP scripts, or databases, then the sky is the limit (or, at least your proficiency with an HTML authoring application is the limit).

Custom .Mac Web pages can be set up to look and feel just about any way you like, and you can host movies and pictures, publish blogs—anything you can do with HTML and static files that you upload to your iDisk.

So, if Apple's templates just aren't doing it for you, it's OK to code your own. A great crash course in HTML Web design is Elizabeth Castro's *Creating a Web Page with HTML: Visual QuickProject Guide* (Peachpit Press, 2004). She also wrote the best-selling *HTML for the World Wide Web with XHTML and CSS: Visual QuickStart Guide, 5th Edition* (Peachpit Press, 2002). In this section of *this* book, however, you'll learn how to integrate a custom-coded Web page into your .Mac account's main page.

Integrating a Custom Site

If you're here, you've taken the time to learn HTML or a graphical editor, and you've created a fabulous site that blows away the already great templates provided by Apple. Now, it's time to take the plunge and put your site up for everyone else to browse.

The benefit of publishing your custom page this way is that your page appears in the list of links at the top of your .Mac site menu (and you optionally get the page counter and contact link). The drawback is that you can't organize it quite as efficiently, and the page is surrounded by the .Mac interface.

Once the custom Web site is uploaded, you can connect to it without doing anything else. Simply point your browser to `http://homepage.mac.com/yourmembername/filename`, where *yourmembername* is your .Mac member name, and *filename* is the name of the index file you've just uploaded.

To integrate a custom site:

1. Gather the HTML files that you'll publish on your .Mac site, along with any supporting files (such as images, Flash animations, or movies), and put them in a folder.

2. Connect to your iDisk, and upload the contents of your site's folder (not the folder itself) to your iDisk's Sites folder. If you upload the whole folder, you can still connect to the site, but you won't be able to use the External HTML template to integrate it into your site (**Figure 4.64**).

3. Log in to your .Mac account using a Web browser, and click the HomePage link.

    The main HomePage page loads.

4. At the bottom of the list of tabs, click the Advanced tab (**Figure 4.65**).

    The Advanced templates page loads, showing one template: External HTML.

Figure 4.64 Drag a custom HTML file to your iDisk's Sites folder to upload that file in preparation for integration into your .Mac site.

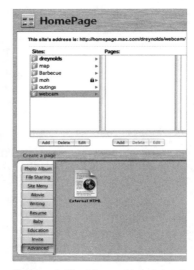

Figure 4.65 The Advanced template tab has one template—External HTML. This template lets you connect an HTML file you create to your .Mac site.

Figure 4.66 When you load the External HTML template, you are asked to locate the HTML document you uploaded. Click it, and then click Choose.

Figure 4.67 After you've loaded the HTML file, the "Edit your page" page loads, allowing you to type a new name for your custom HTML page.

Figure 4.68 After you click the Preview button, the custom page loads as others would see it.

5. Click the External HTML template button.

The "Choose your web page" page loads. The HTML file that you uploaded in step 2 should show up in the Sites folder.

6. Select the HTML file and click Choose (**Figure 4.66**).

The page loads in HomePage in the "Edit your page" page, showing you a preview of how it will look when published.

7. In the title field, type a title for your uploaded page (**Figure 4.67**).

8. If you want a counter or a Send Me a Message link, check the boxes next to these items at the bottom of the page.

9. Click Preview.

A preview of the page loads (**Figure 4.68**).

(continues on next page)

INTEGRATING A CUSTOM SITE

10. If you need to make changes, click Edit. If you're satisfied with how it looks, click Publish.

A page loads with the custom page's URL and gives you the opportunity to send an iCard announcing the new page (**Figure 4.69**).

✔ Tips

■ As long as your links all point to the proper places, you can host a whole Web site, with as many pages, graphics, and supporting files as space on your iDisk will allow.

■ To publish a custom HTML page to a site other than the default site, first create the site using HomePage, and then upload the HTML file (and supporting files) to the proper site folder, which lives in the Sites folder of your iDisk.

Figure 4.69 After you publish the custom HTML page, its URL loads, and you're given the opportunity to send an iCard announcing it.

Forwarding a Domain Name to Your .Mac Site

If you've spent the $10 or so to register your own domain name, you can use your registrar's *domain redirect* function to redirect people to your .Mac site instead. Here's how it works. If people type in

http://www.*yourfancydomain*.com

they're sent to

http://homepage.mac.com/*yourmembername*/index.html.

This process varies a bit from registrar to registrar, but the essential thing to note is that you're simply forwarding your domain to your .Mac site. If you remember that, making changes with your registrar ought to be easy.

Publishing a Custom Site Sans HomePage

If you're a stickler for keeping things organized, there's another way to host your custom site through your .Mac account that doesn't involve HomePage.

Rather than upload the bare Web page and any supporting files for your custom site, upload the folder that contains those pages. There is one major benefit to doing it this way—you can keep your content organized by folder (staying out of the way of the HomePage application). Here's how you go about it.

1. Upload your entire custom site's folder to the Sites folder on your iDisk.

2. Log in to your .Mac account, and click the HomePage link.

3. Rather than clicking the Advanced tab, select the site where you want to include the new custom page, and click the Site Menu tab (**Figure 4.70**). On the new site menu page that results, click the Plus button next to where you'd like a link to your custom site to appear. See the sidebar "Adding Links to Your Site Menu," earlier in this chapter, for complete instructions.

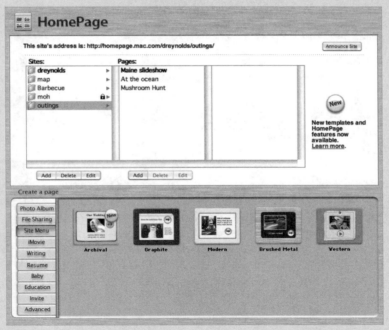

Figure 4.70 To create a new site menu, first select the site where you'd like the menu page to appear in the Sites column, and then click the Site Menu tab below.

(continues on next page)

Publishing a Custom Site Sans HomePage *continued*

4. Give the new link item a proper graphic, title, and description, and then click the Edit Link button.

5. On the "Edit your links" page, click the Other Pages tab, and type in the URL for the index file inside your newly uploaded site folder (such as http://homepage.mac.com/dreynolds/webcam/webcam.html) (**Figure 4.71**).

6. Click Apply.

7. Click Preview to see how the site will look before it goes live. If you like what you see, click Publish.

You can edit an existing site menu page in the same way to include the new site.

Also, here's one tip worth remembering: If you're using this technique, consider naming the index page inside the folder *index.html*. Why? Most Web servers, including the .Mac Web server, are set to automatically serve up the page named index.html if one isn't specified. So, that means that

http://homepage.mac.com/dreynolds/webcam/index.html

and

http://homepage.mac.com/dreynolds/webcam/

work the same. And, hey, you're doing your visitors a favor—a shorter URL means less typing for anyone who wants to visit your site.

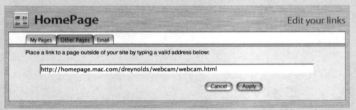

Figure 4.71 Create a link to the newly integrated site by entering its URL in the Other Pages field, and then click Apply.

USING .MAC SYNC

Not only does your .Mac account provide a great ad-free e-mail address, online storage, and the ability to whip up Web pages in a flash, but it also serves as a repository for your personal information—your Safari bookmarks, contacts, calendars, Mail accounts, Mail rules, and keychains (which hold your passwords for various accounts).

There are two great things about this: The first is that when you synchronize these items to your .Mac account, that information can be synchronized with other Macs, so that copying the items to other Macintosh computers is as easy as entering your account information and clicking a button. The second great thing about this is that you can access some of this key information (such as your contacts and Safari bookmarks) from just about any computer with a Web browser and an Internet connection. And, with a little cleverness, you can easily copy your information to a cell phone, iPod, or Palm PDA.

Five software tools allow you to do this. You'll need your .Mac account, iSync, Address Book, Safari, and iCal. All of these come with the latest version of Mac OS X, or they can be downloaded from Apple for older versions of Mac OS X. The sixth important tool—.Mac Sync—is built right into Mac OS X 10.4.

In this chapter, I'll show you how to set up Mac OS X 10.4's .Mac Sync, how to use .Mac Sync to synchronize information between two (or more) Macs using your .Mac account, and how to use iSync to integrate other devices in your synchronization routine.

USING .MAC SYNC

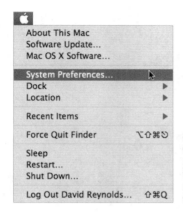

Figure 5.1
Choose System
Preferences
from the Apple
menu to open
the application.

Setting Up .Mac Sync

With the advent of Mac OS X 10.4 Tiger, Apple integrated something called .Mac Sync into the operating system. This simply means that Mac OS X knows how to talk to your .Mac account and share your important information with it. To enable your Mac to do that, you first have to set up the .Mac System Preferences to work properly.

To set up .Mac Sync:

1. From the Apple menu, choose System Preferences (**Figure 5.1**).

   System Preferences launches, and the main System Preferences window opens.

2. Click the .Mac icon in the Internet & Network section (**Figure 5.2**).

   The .Mac pane opens, with the Account tab selected by default (**Figure 5.3**).

   (continues on next page)

Figure 5.2 Click the .Mac icon to load the .Mac preferences.

Figure 5.3 The .Mac pane opens, by default, to the Account tab.

3. Make sure your .Mac member name and password are entered in the .Mac Member Name and Password fields, respectively.

4. Click the Sync tab.

The .Mac Sync preferences load (**Figure 5.4**).

5. At the top of the pane, check the Synchronize with .Mac check box. This turns .Mac synchronization on.

6. From the Synchronize with .Mac pop-up menu, choose whether you want synchronizations to take place automatically, every hour, every day, every week, or manually (**Figure 5.5**).

7. Check the boxes next to the items you want synchronized. Your choices are Bookmarks, Calendars, Contacts, Keychains, Mail Accounts, and Mail Rules, Signatures, and Smart Mailboxes (for a rundown on each of these, see the sidebar "What .Mac Sync Synchronizes").

8. If you want to have the Sync icon appear in the menu bar, check the "Show status in menu bar" check box at the bottom of the window.

Figure 5.4 Clicking the Sync tab opens the .Mac Sync preferences, where you can control what is synchronized, and when.

Figure 5.5 From the pop-up menu, you can choose whether synchronizations happen automatically, hourly, daily, weekly, or manually.

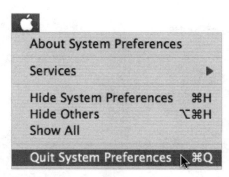

Figure 5.6 From the System Preferences menu, choose Quit System Preferences to quit the application and save your changes.

9. From the System Preferences menu, choose Quit (Command-Q) to quit System Preferences and save your .Mac sync changes (**Figure 5.6**).

✔ **Tip**

■ You can click the Sync Now button at the bottom of the .Mac Sync preferences window to perform a synchronization at any time.

What .Mac Sync Synchronizes

You may be curious about what each of those check boxes in the .Mac Sync preferences represents. After all, it's good to know what information gets synchronized to your .Mac account. Here's a rundown:

◆ **Bookmarks**—Your Safari bookmarks

◆ **Calendars**—Your iCal calendars

◆ **Contacts**—Your Address Book contact information

◆ **Keychains**—Your Keychain-managed login information (including passwords)

◆ **Mail Accounts**—Your Mail account information for all accounts

◆ **Mail Rules, Signatures, and Smart Mailboxes**—Rules, signatures, and any Smart Mailboxes that you've set up

Performing Your First Sync

The first time you synchronize your computer with your .Mac account is different from other synchronizations—you have to make some choices about how things will proceed during the synchronization. Mostly, you have to decide whether information will be merged or replaced—and, if it's being replaced, whether that replacement takes place on the computer or in the .Mac account.

To perform your first sync:

1. In the .Mac Sync System Preferences, set up a sync and click Sync Now (**Figure 5.7**).

   An alert window opens, asking what you would like to do for this first sync (**Figure 5.8**).

2. From the only pop-up menu in the alert window, *choose one of the following* (**Figure 5.9**):

   ▲ **Merge data on this computer and .Mac**—This choice, selected by default, does its best to merge the information on your Mac with that in your .Mac account.

   ▲ **Replace data on .Mac**—This choice replaces the information in your .Mac account with the information on your Mac. Choose this when you want to have the information on your computer be the starting point for all synchronizations. Remember—choosing this option will erase all of the synchronized information in your .Mac account for the category listed in the dialog.

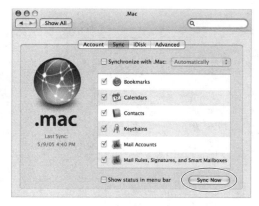

Figure 5.7 Clicking the Sync Now button causes a synchronization to happen immediately.

Figure 5.8 The first time you perform a synchronization, an alert pops up asking you how you want to handle the data transfer.

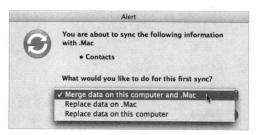

Figure 5.9 From the pop-up menu, choose whether you'd like to merge data or replace it in one place or another.

Figure 5.10 If you're synchronizing conflicting information when merging data—such as two contacts with the same name but different addresses—the Conflict Resolver dialog appears.

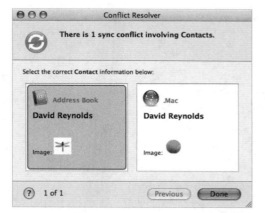

Figure 5.11 When making a choice between two conflicting bits of data, the choice is presented clearly in the Conflict Resolver dialog. Simply click the information that's correct to keep it.

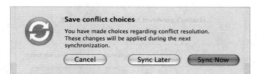

Figure 5.12 After you've made your selection in each conflict, the "Save conflict choices" dialog opens, asking you to synchronize your information again. Click the Sync Now button to perform another sync.

▲ **Replace data on this computer—** This choice replaces the information on your Mac with the information in your .Mac account. Choose this when you want to use the information in your .Mac account as the starting point for all synchronizations. This is especially useful when you want to set up a new computer with your .Mac data without having to reenter contact information, Safari bookmarks, or Mail accounts.

3. Click Sync.

   Your Mac begins synchronizing its information with your .Mac account. If you're merging information and there is conflicting data, the Conflict Resolver dialog opens, and you're given the choice of reviewing information now or later (**Figure 5.10**). The dialog also tells you how many data points conflict, so you can make a choice.

4. Click Review Now.

   The Conflict Resolver dialog expands to show the "Select the correct information" section, where the two pieces of conflicting information appear side by side (**Figure 5.11**).

5. Click the side with the correct information to resolve the conflict.

   If there is more than one conflict, the next one loads in the dialog. Choose the correct information for each by clicking the proper side. When you've gone through all of the conflicts, the "Save conflict choices" dialog appears, noting that the changes will be applied the next time you perform a synchronization (**Figure 5.12**).

   (continues on next page)

6. Click Sync Now.

Your Mac synchronizes its information with your .Mac account, resolving the conflicts as you directed.

✔ Tips

■ When you perform a .Mac synchronization for the first time, you may be presented with the first sync dialog a couple of times—separating your contacts from your Mail accounts, rules, signature, smart mailboxes, and keychains. The process is the same; this separation just allows you to do something different with your contacts than you do with the other data.

■ Conflicting information can be as major as entirely different phone numbers and addresses for a given contact, or it can be as simple as conflicting images associated with an account. If you see the Conflict Resolver dialog open, don't panic—it often means minor adjustments.

Figure 5.13 Clicking the Sync Now button forces a synchronization to happen immediately.

Figure 5.14 If you elected to have Sync in the menu bar, you can perform a synchronization at any time by selecting Sync Now from that menu.

Performing a Manual Sync

If you've set up your .Mac Sync preferences to Automatic, Every Hour, Every Day, or Every Week, your computer will automatically synchronize your data on the schedule you've set. If you've set it to Manually, however, you'll have to be the one to initiate a sync.

To manually perform a sync:

1. From the Apple menu, choose System Preferences.

The System Preferences application launches, and the main System Preferences window opens.

2. Click the .Mac icon.

The .Mac pane opens, with the Account tab selected.

3. Click the Sync tab.

The .Mac Sync preferences load.

4. In the lower right corner of the .Mac Sync preferences, click the Sync Now button (**Figure 5.13**).

Your Mac synchronizes your information with your .Mac account.

✔ Tip

■ If you've checked the "Show status in menu bar" check box, you can choose Sync Now from the Sync menu to initiate a sync (**Figure 5.14**).

Unregistering a Mac

When you perform a synchronization to your .Mac account, the Mac that performs the synchronization is automatically registered with your .Mac account. If you sell your Mac or otherwise don't want to use it with your .Mac account, you can unregister it from your .Mac account, so that it's no longer eligible for synchronization.

To unregister a Mac:

1. From the Apple menu, choose System Preferences.

   The System Preferences application launches, and the main System Preferences window opens.

2. Click the .Mac icon.

   The .Mac pane opens, with the Account tab selected.

3. Click the Advanced tab.

   The .Mac Advanced preferences load, showing all computers registered to be synchronized with your .Mac account (**Figure 5.15**).

4. From the Registered Computer list, select the computer that you want to unregister and click the Unregister button.

   A sheet slides down, asking if you're sure that you want to unregister the selected computer (**Figure 5.16**).

5. Click Unregister.

   After a short wait, the selected computer is unregistered and no longer appears in the list (**Figure 5.17**).

6. From the System Preferences menu, choose Quit (Command-Q) to quit System Preferences and save your .Mac sync changes.

   System Preferences quits.

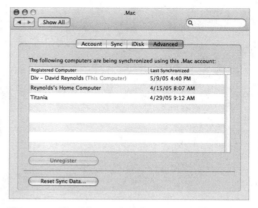

Figure 5.15 The Advanced tab lets you control which computers are authorized to synchronize with your .Mac account, as well as reset synchronization data.

Figure 5.16 Before you're allowed to unregister a computer, a sheet slides down to ask if you're sure—and to warn you of the consequences (which are minor). Click Unregister.

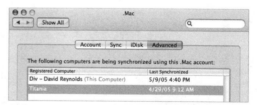

Figure 5.17 After you unregister a computer, it no longer appears in the Registered Computer list.

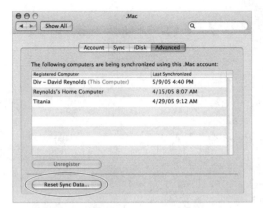

Figure 5.18 The Reset Sync Data button allows you to "take back" the last synchronization you've done, by replacing the synchronized data with a copy.

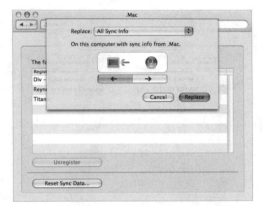

Figure 5.19 When the Reset Sync Data button is clicked, a sheet slides down presenting you with some options on what data to replace and where. Choose what data to replace from the pop-up menu, and click either the left or right arrow underneath to choose where the data is replaced.

Resetting Sync Data

You can reset the .Mac sync data whenever you have an Internet connection, so that the data on your Mac matches the information in your .Mac account, or vice versa—useful if you don't want to keep the changes that were made with your last sync.

To reset your sync data:

1. From the Apple menu, choose System Preferences.

   The System Preferences application launches, and the main System Preferences window opens.

2. Click the .Mac icon.

   The .Mac pane opens, with the Account tab selected.

3. Click the Advanced tab.

   The .Mac Advanced preferences load, showing all computers registered to be synchronized with your .Mac account.

4. Click the Reset Sync Data button (**Figure 5.18**).

   A sheet slides down, asking for specifics on which information to reset, and what to use as the replacement source, indicated by two arrows (**Figure 5.19**).

(continues on next page)

5. From the Replace pop-up menu at the top of the sheet, *choose one of the following to reset* (**Figure 5.20**):

▲ **All Sync Info**—This replaces all information.

▲ **Bookmarks**—This replaces just your Safari bookmarks.

▲ **Calendars**—This replaces just your calendar information.

▲ **Contacts**—This replaces just your contact information.

▲ **Keychains**—This replaces just your keychain information.

▲ **Mail Accounts**—This replaces just your Mail account information.

▲ **Mail Rules, Signatures, and Smart Mailboxes**—This replaces just the Mail rules, signatures, and any Smart Mailboxes (mailboxes created using a Spotlight search) you've created.

6. Click one of the arrow buttons to choose whether information is replaced on the computer or on the .Mac account (**Figure 5.21**).

Clicking the left arrow replaces information on the computer with information from the .Mac account. Clicking the right arrow replaces information on the .Mac account with information from the computer.

7. Click Replace.

The information is replaced as specified during the next synchronization.

Figure 5.20 The Replace pop-up menu allows you to choose which data you want to replace—including replacing all data.

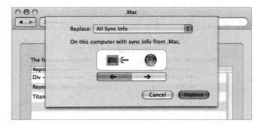

Figure 5.21 Click the arrow to indicate which source to use as replacement data, and then click the Replace button to start the synchronization.

RESETTING SYNC DATA

Figure 5.22 The iSync window starts out with just one icon—the one labeled .mac.

Figure 5.23 To add a device to iSync, choose Add Device from the Device menu or press Command-N.

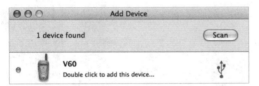

Figure 5.24 When an eligible device is found, the Add Device window expands to provide details. In this case, iSync has discovered a V60 cell phone connected by USB.

Synchronizing with a Phone

Mac OS X 10.4 comes with a utility program called iSync, which lets you synchronize some of your information to other handheld devices, such as cell phones and iPods—in addition to your .Mac account.

To use iSync with a cell phone:

1. Connect your cell phone to your Mac via USB or Bluetooth.

2. In the Applications folder, double-click iSync to launch it.

   The iSync window opens (**Figure 5.22**). By default, it has one lonely little icon— the .mac icon.

3. From the Devices menu, choose Add Device (Command-N) (**Figure 5.23**).

   The Add Device window opens, and iSync scans for any eligible connected devices. When it finds one, it notifies you in the Add Device window (**Figure 5.24**).

4. Double-click the found device to add it to iSync.

   iSync adds the device and shows its preferences (**Figure 5.25**). The preferences in this window vary according to the specific model of device you've connected.

   (continues on next page)

5. From the "For first sync" pop-up menu, *choose one of the following:*

   ▲ "Merge data on computer and device" to preserve data on both the phone and your Mac, merging it and reporting any conflicting data to you.

   ▲ "Erase data on device then sync" to erase the phone data and replace its data with information from your Mac.

6. Check the "Turn on synchronization" box. This ensures that the device has its data synchronized.

7. Check the boxes next to the information you want synchronized. This varies depending on the device, but it can include contact information, calendar events, and to-do items.

8. In the upper right corner of the iSync window, click the Sync Devices button.

   iSync synchronizes information between your phone, your Mac, and your .Mac account (**Figure 5.26**).

✔ Tips

- Not all cell phones work with iSync. To check if your phone is compatible, visit http://www.apple.com/macosx/features/isync/devices.html.

- If you're using a Bluetooth phone, be sure that it has been set up through the Bluetooth section of System Preferences before you set up iSync to work with it.

- The .Mac icon in iSync 2.0 doesn't do much—it presents a dialog noting that you have to change your .Mac sync preferences in the .Mac section of System Preferences. That dialog has a button called Open .Mac Preferences, which, if clicked, opens the .Mac section of System Preferences.

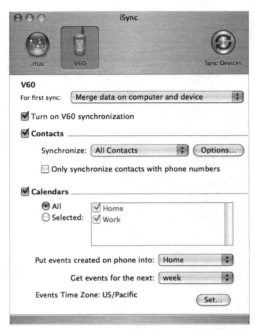

Figure 5.25 After a device has been added, its preferences are displayed. These preferences differ, based on the kind and model of device detected.

Figure 5.26 iSync presents a progress bar when information is being synchronized between your computer, a device, and your .Mac account.

Figure 5.27 When iSync is launched after a device is added, the device's icon appears in the main iSync window.

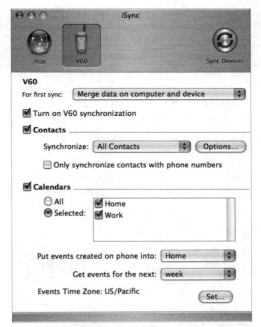

Figure 5.28 Before a device can be removed from iSync, its icon must be selected, which causes the window to expand, showing the device's preferences.

Removing a Device from iSync

iSync allows you to remove a device you previously added, so that it's no longer synchronized—say, you give your iPod to your kid or you upgrade your cell phone and need to remove the old one.

To remove a device from iSync:

1. Physically connect the device to your Mac via USB, FireWire, or Bluetooth.

2. In the Applications folder, double-click iSync to launch it.

   The iSync window opens (**Figure 5.27**).

3. Click the icon of the device you want to remove.

   The window expands to show the device's preferences (**Figure 5.28**).

   (continues on next page)

4. From the Devices menu, choose Remove Device (**Figure 5.29**).

A dialog opens asking if you want to remove the device from iSync (**Figure 5.30**).

5. Click OK.

The device is removed from iSync (**Figure 5.31**).

Figure 5.29 To remove a device, choose Remove Device from the Devices menu.

Figure 5.30 Before you're allowed to remove a device from iSync, you're asked to confirm the action. Click OK.

Figure 5.31 After the device is removed, the iSync window returns to its previous size—minus the removed device's icon.

iSync for Mac OS X 10.2 or 10.3

Mac OS X 10.2 and 10.3 do not have built-in .Mac synchronization capabilities. But if you don't have Mac OS X 10.4, don't despair. You can download a version of iSync that works with Mac OS X 10.2 and 10.3.

This version of iSync (version 1.5) works with some cell phones and iPods, and it also controls how your Mac synchronizes its information with your .Mac account. With iSync 1.5, all synchronization is done with iSync.

You can download iSync 1.5 at www.apple.com/support/downloads/isync.html.

Setting .Mac iSync Preferences

iSync has a number of preferences you can set to control how your computer, your .Mac account, and any devices that you've set up share information (**Figure 5.32**). To access the iSync preferences, choose Preferences from the iSync menu.

Here's what each preference does:

◆ **Enable syncing on this computer**—With this check box you turn synchronization on and off for this computer, as well as for your .Mac account.

◆ **Show HotSync reminder when syncing Palm OS devices**—If you're using a Palm OS–based device, with this check box you tell iSync to show the HotSync reminder when you use iSync with it.

◆ **Show status in menu bar**—This check box allows you to have the Sync menu appear in the menu bar.

◆ **Show Data Change Alert when**—This pop-up menu lets you set how much of your personal information can be changed before an alert pops up. By default, an alert appears if more than 5 percent of the data on your computer changes during a synchronization (**Figure 5.33**).

◆ **Reset Sync History**—You click this button to reset the Mac's synchronization history, which effectively wipes the slate clean. After you reset your sync history, the computer behaves as if it were the first time a synchronization had taken place. See "Performing Your First Sync" for more on what happens during a first synchronization.

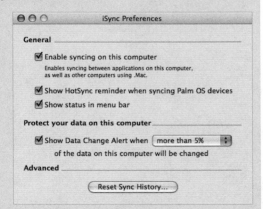

Figure 5.32 iSync's preferences allow you some control over how iSync behaves.

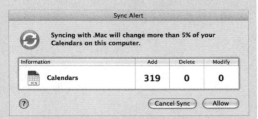

Figure 5.33 If more than a certain amount of information will be changed by a synchronization, an alert window provides some details on what's happening—including what's being changed; how many items are being added, deleted, or modified; and whether the synchronization should be allowed or canceled.

USING ADDRESS BOOK

6

In Chapter 5, "Using .Mac Sync," we covered how to turn on .Mac Sync and synchronize your bookmarks, calendars, contacts, keychains, and mail accounts with your .Mac account. Once you've done that, you're ready to start tapping in to one of .Mac's most powerful features—the ability to access all of that luscious contact information from anywhere in the world using a Web browser and an Internet connection.

After you've performed a synchronization, you can look up contact information in your .Mac Address Book from any computer, and you can also use those contacts to quickly address e-mail messages from within .Mac's Webmail interface.

In this chapter, I'll show you how to set Address Book preferences, add and remove contacts from Address Book, and browse and search through the contact information stored in your .Mac Address Book using a Web browser. I'll also explain how to edit contacts and share the contact information stored in your Mac OS X 10.4 Tiger Address Book with others.

An important note: In this chapter, we're talking about two separate things with the same name. Your Mac OS X Address Book is an application that lets you store and organize contact information; your .Mac Address Book is where you store contact information in your .Mac account. Through Mac OS X synchronization, you can keep the information in your Mac OS X Address Book and .Mac Address Book in sync.

USING ADDRESS BOOK

Figure 6.1 After you've logged in to your .Mac account, your .Mac member name appears in the upper right corner of the page.

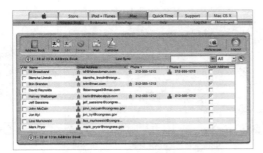

Figure 6.2 When you open your .Mac Address Book, the contacts are listed in groups of ten, and a toolbar appears at the top of the page. Click the Preferences button to open the Preferences page.

Setting .Mac Address Book Preferences

Your .Mac Address Book allows you to set some preferences that govern how it behaves. By changing these preferences, you can select the number of contacts that are displayed per page, change how addresses are sorted, choose the defaults for the kind of data you enter, and turn on (or off) Address Book Synchronization.

To set .Mac Address Book preferences:

1. At www.mac.com, log in to your .Mac account.

   The main .Mac welcome page opens, with you logged in (**Figure 6.1**).

2. Click the Address Book link at the top of the page or in the left column of the page.

   The main .Mac Address Book page opens, listing your contacts and their e-mail addresses and phone numbers (**Figure 6.2**).

(continues on next page)

SETTING .MAC ADDRESS BOOK PREFERENCES

3. Click the Preferences button at the top of the .Mac Address Book page.

The .Mac Address Book preferences page opens (**Figure 6.3**). On this page, you can see how many contacts are in your .Mac Address Book, and you can set how it behaves.

4. On the .Mac Address Book preferences page, *do the following*:

▲ Select the number of contacts to be displayed per page from the Contacts Per Page pop-up menu.

▲ Select whether addresses are sorted by last name or first name from the Display Order pop-up menu.

▲ Choose whether Home or Work is set as the default e-mail address in the Default Email pop-up menu.

▲ Choose whether Home, Work, Mobile, or Fax is set as the default phone number in the Default Phone #1 pop-up menu.

▲ Choose whether Home, Work, Mobile, or Fax is set as the default phone number in the Default Phone #2 pop-up menu.

▲ Choose whether Email, Last Name, or First Name is set as the default sort order in the Default Sort Order pop-up menu.

▲ Check the Turn on .Mac Address Book Synchronization box to turn on Address Book synchronization (as covered in Chapter 5).

5. Click Save.

Your preferences are saved, and the main Address Book page opens.

✔ Tip

■ You can go right to your .Mac Address Book by pointing your Web browser to http://addressbook.mac.com (there's no www). If this is the first time you've accessed your Address Book via .Mac and you've already performed a sync, you may be told that you'll have to perform an additional sync—this time from your .Mac account to your computer.

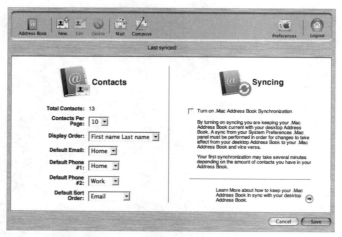

Figure 6.3 The .Mac Address Book preferences page lets you set how your .Mac Address Book behaves.

Figure 6.4 The .Mac Web Address Book also lists contacts in groups of ten, and it provides a toolbar with some common commands for your use.

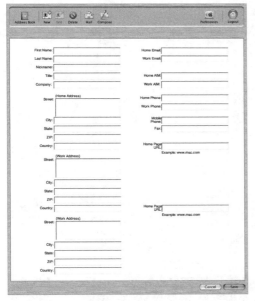

Figure 6.5 When you click the New button in the toolbar, the new-contact page opens. On it, you can enter as much contact information as you like.

Adding Contacts to Address Book

.Mac does a fabulous job of pulling updated information from your local Address Book application that comes with Mac OS X through .Mac Sync (as described in Chapter 5). It's not the only way to add contact information to your .Mac account, though. You can also add contacts using your Web browser.

To add a contact using a Web browser:

1. Log in to your .Mac Address Book.

   The main .Mac Address Book page opens (**Figure 6.4**).

2. In the toolbar at the top of the page, click the New button.

   The new-contact page opens (**Figure 6.5**).

3. In the fields on the new-contact page, enter as much of the following information as you like:

   ▲ Personal information, such as first name, last name, title, and company

   ▲ Physical addresses for work and home

   ▲ E-mail addresses for work and home

   ▲ AIM account information for work and home

   ▲ Telephone numbers for work, home, mobile phone, and fax

   ▲ URL for the contact's homepage

   (continues on next page)

ADDING CONTACTS TO ADDRESS BOOK

4. Click Save (**Figure 6.6**).

You are returned to the main .Mac Address Book page. The new contact shows in the contact list (**Figure 6.7**). The next time you sync your Mac, the new contact information will also be downloaded to your computer's Mac OS X Address Book application. If you add a contact and immediately synchronize, however, you may not see the changes right away. Wait a few minutes and try synchronizing again.

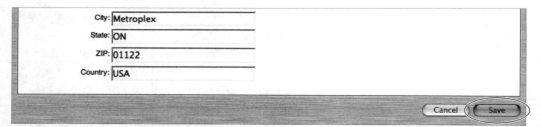

Figure 6.6 After you've entered the contact information, click Save.

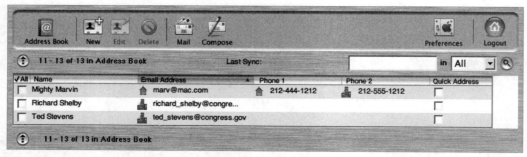

Figure 6.7 The new contact appears in your .Mac Address Book in your .Mac account.

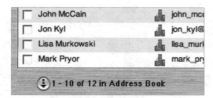

Figure 6.8 To see the next set of ten contacts, click the downward-pointing arrow.

Figure 6.9 The detailed information page for a given contact contains as much information as you've entered, but it *can* include name; work and home addresses; work and home e-mail addresses; work, home, mobile, and fax numbers; Web-site URLs, and more.

Viewing Contact Information

When you log in to your .Mac Address Book at www.mac.com, a page opens displaying a list of your contacts. If you don't have a lot of contacts, you might just want to browse through the list until you find the person you need to reach. When your contacts start to number in the hundreds, however, performing a search for the person you need to get in touch with will save you time.

To browse contact information:

1. Log in to your .Mac Address Book.

    The main .Mac Address Book page opens, listing your contacts and their e-mail addresses and phone numbers.

2. In the lower left corner of the page, click the downward-pointing arrow to bring up the next set of ten addresses (**Figure 6.8**).

    The next set of ten addresses appears.

3. Click a name, e-mail address, or phone number to bring up the detailed information for that contact.

    The contact's detailed information page opens (**Figure 6.9**).

✔ Tip

- You can also browse up through your addresses ten at a time by clicking the upward-pointing arrow at the bottom of the addresses (assuming you're not viewing the first set of ten).

To search contact information:

1. Log in to your .Mac Address Book. The main .Mac Address Book page opens.

2. In the upper right corner of the Address Book page, type your search terms. They can be names, e-mail addresses, or phone numbers.

3. From the "in" pop-up menu, choose the criterion you want to use to restrict your search (if you want to use any). The default choice is All; you can restrict your search to names, e-mail addresses, or phone numbers (**Figure 6.10**).

4. Click the magnifying glass button to conduct the search.

   The search results page appears, showing you all the matches (**Figure 6.11**).

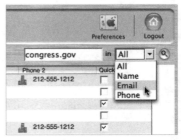

Figure 6.10 If you want to restrict your search to just names, e-mail addresses, or phone numbers, you can do so by selecting the appropriate criterion from the "in" pop-up menu.

Figure 6.11 Once the search is complete, its results are displayed in a list.

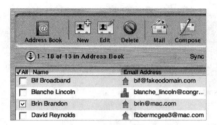

Figure 6.12 Check the box to the left of the address you want to edit.

Figure 6.13 When the contact-editing page opens, you can make any changes you like to the selected contact's information. Click Save to save your changes.

Editing Contact Information

At times, you may need to change a contact's information—say you've misspelled an e-mail address, you need to use it for a series of messages, and you don't feel much like correcting it every time.

To edit contact information:

1. Log in to your .Mac Address Book.

   The main .Mac Address Book page opens.

2. Check the box to the left of the contact you want to edit (**Figure 6.12**). You can edit only one contact at a time.

3. At the top of the page, click the Edit button.

   The contact-editing page opens (**Figure 6.13**).

4. Make any necessary changes to the contact's information and click Save.

   Your changes are saved, and the main .Mac Address Book page opens.

To delete a contact:

1. Log in to your .Mac Address Book.

   The main .Mac Address Book page opens.

2. Check the boxes to the left of all the contacts you want to delete (**Figure 6.14**). You can delete more than one contact at a time.

3. Click the Delete button.

   A page appears, asking if you're sure you want to delete the selected contacts (**Figure 6.15**).

4. If you're sure you want to delete the contacts, click Yes.

   The selected contacts are deleted and the main Address Book page opens.

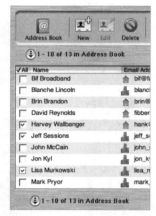

Figure 6.14 Check the boxes next to the contacts you want to delete.

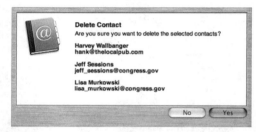

Figure 6.15 Before any contacts are deleted, you are asked if you want to go through with the deletion. Click Yes to continue.

Figure 6.16 The first step to sharing an address book is to open the Address Book application.

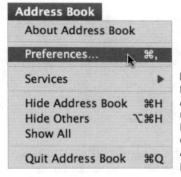

Figure 6.17 From the Address Book menu, choose Preferences to open the Address Book preferences.

Figure 6.18 The Address Book preferences window is where you make changes to how the local version of Address Book behaves; it's also where you set up Address Book sharing.

Sharing Address Book Information

Mac OS X 10.4 has an updated version of Address Book with one great new feature: Address Book sharing. With this feature, you can share your Address Book contacts with anyone who has a .Mac account, and you can choose whether those people can edit your contacts, or just read them. If someone has listed your .Mac account in his or her authorized list of Address Book sharers, you can subscribe to that person's information from Address Book.

To share your Address Book information:

1. In the Applications folder, double-click the Address Book icon to open the application.

   The main Address Book window opens (**Figure 6.16**).

2. From the Address Book menu, choose Preferences (**Figure 6.17**).

   The Address Book preferences window opens to the General pane by default (**Figure 6.18**).

(continues on next page)

3. At the top of the window, click the Sharing button.

The Sharing pane opens (**Figure 6.19**).

4. Check the "Share your Address Book" box.

Address Book sets up sharing behind the scenes over the course of a few seconds.

5. In the lower left corner of the Sharing pane, click the plus (+) button.

A sheet listing Address Book contacts slides down (**Figure 6.20**).

6. Select the .Mac member or members with whom you want to share your Address Book information and click OK.

The sheet slides back up, and the selected contact can access your Address Book information (**Figure 6.21**).

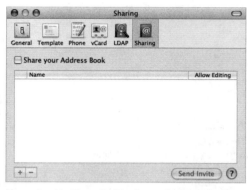

Figure 6.19 You'll use the Sharing preferences pane to control who can access your Address Book information.

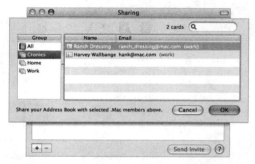

Figure 6.20 When you click the plus (+) button in the Sharing pane, a sheet listing the available Address Book contacts slides down. Select a .Mac member with whom you want to share your Address Book information and click OK.

Figure 6.21 Once you've added a .Mac member to the sharing list, that person's name appears in the Sharing pane.

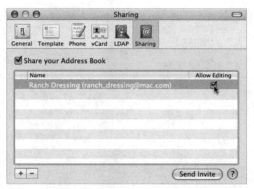

Figure 6.22 Checking the Allow Editing check box to the right of a .Mac member's name enables that member to edit your contact information.

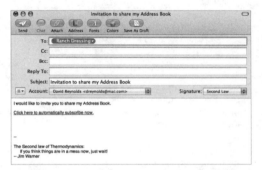

Figure 6.23 When you click Send Invite, an e-mail message is automatically generated in your default e-mail program. This message is addressed to the person who is authorized to share your Address Book information.

7. If you want to allow the .Mac member to edit your Address Book information, check the Allow Editing check box to the right of the name (**Figure 6.22**).

8. If you want to send an e-mail invitation to the .Mac member with whom you're sharing your Address Book information, click the Send Invite button in the lower right corner of the Sharing preferences pane.

A new e-mail with an invitation and a link to subscribe to your Address Book is generated in your default e-mail program (**Figure 6.23**). Send it when you're ready.

9. Click the red close button in the upper left corner of the Sharing preferences pane to close the window—and save your changes.

✔ Tip

■ To remove someone from your authorized list of those who can share your Address Book information, click the minus (–) button in the lower left corner of the Sharing preferences pane.

To subscribe to another .Mac member's Address Book:

1. In the Applications folder, double-click the Address Book icon to open the application.

The main Address Book window opens.

2. From the File menu, choose Subscribe to Address Book (**Figure 6.24**).

A sheet slides down asking for the account information of the .Mac member to whose Address Book information you want to subscribe.

3. Type the e-mail address for the .Mac member in the "Subscribe to this .Mac member's Address Book" field (**Figure 6.25**).

4. Click OK.

The .Mac member's Address Book appears in the lower left corner of the main Address Book window—in the Group column (**Figure 6.26**). Click the .Mac member's name to open the address book.

✔ Tip

■ To unsubscribe from another member's .Mac Address Book information, select the address book from which you want to unsubscribe in the main Address Book window, and then press the Delete key.

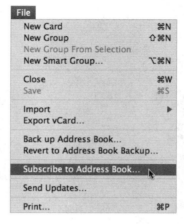

Figure 6.24 Choose Subscribe to Address Book from Address Book's File menu to begin the subscription process.

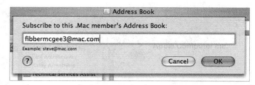

Figure 6.25 Address Book asks for the e-mail address of the .Mac member to whose Address Book information you want to subscribe. Type in the e-mail address and click OK.

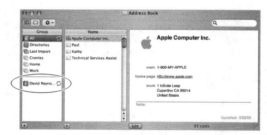

Figure 6.26 Once you've subscribed to a .Mac member's Address Book, it appears in the left column of the main Address Book window.

USING .MAC BOOKMARKS

If you use Safari as your Web browser, you can take advantage of one of .Mac's nifty information-synchronization features: the ability to keep a common set of browser bookmarks among several different Macs, *and* have those bookmarks available online from just about any Web browser.

This synchronization of bookmarks is a real time- and frustration-saver if you have more than one Mac, as anyone who's ever tried to keep bookmarks organized between two or more machines knows.

It's also a real boon for those who travel without the benefit of being able to take their main computers with them. With .Mac bookmark synchronization, your bookmarks are never any farther away than a Web browser and an Internet connection.

The only drawback with .Mac Bookmarks is that you have to use Safari in order to take advantage of them—too bad for the Firefox, Camino, Opera, Microsoft Internet Explorer, Netscape Navigator, Mozilla, and OmniWeb users among us.

In this chapter, I'll show you how to access your Safari bookmarks using a Web browser, add a bookmark, and remove bookmarks and folders. I'll also show you how to set your preferences so that your bookmarks behave the way you want them to.

Accessing Your .Mac Bookmarks

Once you have .Mac synchronization set up properly—as explained in Chapter 5, "Using .Mac Sync"—and you've synchronized your bookmarks, calendars, contacts, keychains, and mail information between your Macintosh and your .Mac account, the bookmarks from Safari on your synchronized computer will be available through your .Mac account, waiting for you to use them.

To access your .Mac Bookmarks:

1. At www.mac.com, log in to your .Mac account (**Figure 7.1**).

   The main .Mac welcome page opens, with you logged in (**Figure 7.2**).

Figure 7.1 Enter your .Mac member name and password in the respective fields, and then click Enter to log in to .Mac.

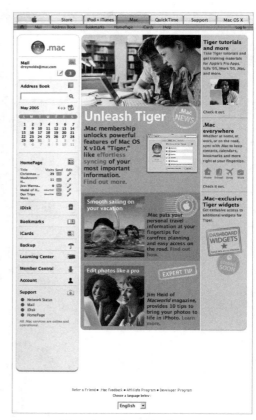

Figure 7.2 This is the main .Mac welcome page, which shows me as being logged in.

ACCESSING YOUR .MAC BOOKMARKS

Figure 7.3 Click the Bookmarks link at the top of the page.

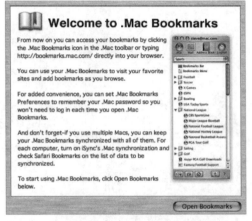

Figure 7.4 The Welcome to .Mac Bookmarks page gives you basic information on how to use .Mac bookmarks, as well as how to synchronize them.

2. At the top of the page, click the Bookmarks link (**Figure 7.3**).

The Welcome to .Mac Bookmarks page opens (**Figure 7.4**). The first time you visit the .Mac Bookmarks page, you may be notified that your bookmarks will be synchronized. This is OK.

3. At the bottom of the page, click the Open Bookmarks button.

Your .Mac Bookmarks window opens, listing the Safari bookmarks synchronized with your computer (**Figure 7.5**). The original browser reloads the main .Mac members' page.

4. To use these bookmarks, click one.

A new browser window opens and loads the Web site of the clicked bookmark (**Figure 7.6**).

(continues on next page)

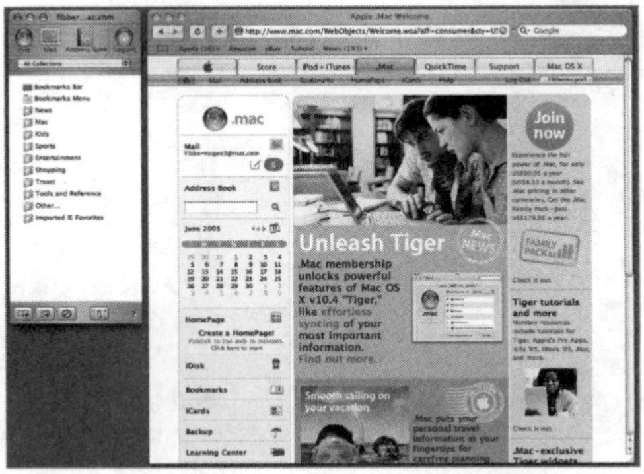

Figure 7.5 The .Mac Bookmarks window loads as a separate browser window that can be conveniently pulled to the side of your main browser window.

Figure 7.6 When you click a bookmark in the .Mac Bookmarks window, a new full-size browser window opens and loads the Web site of the clicked bookmark.

ACCESSING YOUR .MAC BOOKMARKS

5. To open a collection (one of the items indicated by a folder icon), click its icon in the .Mac Bookmarks window (**Figure 7.7**). Don't let the term *collection* throw you—it's really just a top-level folder to help organize your bookmarks.

The collection's contents are loaded in the window (**Figure 7.8**). This can include folders and bookmarks.

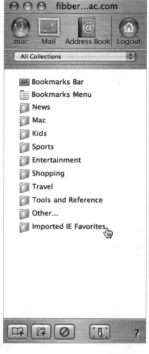

Figure 7.7 Click the icon of a collection (one of the items with the folder icon) to open it and load its contents.

Figure 7.8 Bookmark collections can contain folders or bookmarks, or a mix of the two.

Figure 7.9 When you click the icon for a folder, its contents are listed for your use, and the triangle to the left of the folder's name points down.

Figure 7.10 To load a different .Mac Bookmarks collection, choose its name from the pop-up menu at the top of the .Mac Bookmarks window.

6. To open a folder, click it.

The disclosure triangle to the left of the folder icon rotates to point down, and the folder's contents are listed in the window (**Figure 7.9**).

7. To view another .Mac Bookmarks collection, choose its name from the pop-up menu below the toolbar (**Figure 7.10**). The selected collection loads.

✔ Tips

- You can also load your .Mac Bookmarks by going to http://bookmarks.mac.com using a Web browser.

- You can quickly access other areas of your .Mac account by clicking the .Mac, Mail, and Address Book buttons at the top of your .Mac Bookmarks window.

- To open the Help page for .Mac Bookmarks, click the question mark in the lower right corner of the window.

Adding a Bookmark

If you're browsing the Web on someone else's computer, and you run across a site that you really want to bookmark, you can use your .Mac account and a Web browser to add that bookmark to your .Mac Bookmarks.

Of course, if you're working on your own computer, you can simply add the bookmark to Safari and it will appear in your .Mac Bookmarks the next time you synchronize your Mac with your .Mac account.

To add a bookmark to your .Mac Bookmarks:

1. Open your .Mac Bookmarks window.

   Your .Mac Bookmarks window opens as shown in Figure 7.5.

2. In the lower left corner of the window, click the Add Bookmark button (**Figure 7.11**). The Add Bookmark button looks like an open book with a plus (+) sign on it.

   The bottom portion of the window expands to show the Add Bookmark fields (**Figure 7.12**).

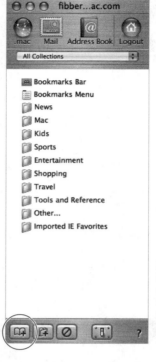

Figure 7.11 The Add Bookmark button, at the bottom of the window, is a quick way to add a bookmark to your .Mac Bookmarks.

Figure 7.12 When you click the Add Bookmark button, fields appear where you can add a bookmark name, URL, and location for your new bookmark.

Figure 7.13 After you've filled in the relevant fields for your new bookmark, click the Add button to create it.

3. In the Add Bookmark fields, *do the following* (**Figure 7.13**):

▲ In the Bookmark Name field, type in a short descriptive name for the new bookmark.

▲ In the Bookmark URL field, type in the URL for the Web page you want to bookmark.

▲ From the Add Bookmark To pop-up menu, select the collection to which you want to add the bookmark.

4. Click the Add button.

The .Mac Bookmarks page reloads, complete with the new bookmark; you may have to open a collection to see your new addition, depending on where you saved it (**Figure 7.14**). The next time you synchronize, your new bookmark will be added to Safari in the collection you specified.

Figure 7.14 Your newly added bookmark appears in the collection you specified, ready for your use.

ADDING A BOOKMARK

Adding a Bookmark Folder

Although you can't use the .Mac Web site to do full bookmark management—that is, you can't rename, move, or copy bookmarks or folders using it—you *can* perform some rudimentary organization by creating folders for bookmarks.

To add a .Mac Bookmarks folder:

1. Open your .Mac Bookmarks window.

2. At the bottom of the window, click the Add Folder button (**Figure 7.15**). The Add Folder button looks like a file folder with a plus (+) sign on it.

   The bottom portion of the window expands to show the Add Folder options (**Figure 7.16**).

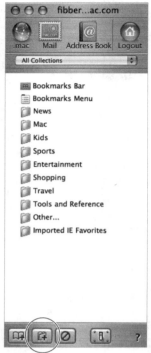

Figure 7.15 The Add Folder button, at the bottom of the window, lets you quickly add a folder for new bookmarks.

Figure 7.16 When you click the Add Folder button, a field and a pop-up menu appear, allowing you to enter a name and choose a location for your new folder.

Figure 7.17 After you've filled in the relevant information for your new bookmark, click Add to create it.

3. In the Add Folder options, *do the following* (**Figure 7.17**):

▲ In the Folder Name field, type in a short descriptive name for the new folder.

▲ From the Add Folder To pop-up menu, choose the collection (or folder within a collection) to which you want to add the folder.

4. Click Add.

The .Mac Bookmarks window reloads, complete with the new folder; you may have to open a collection or folders within a collection to see your new creation, depending on where you created it (**Figure 7.18**).

✔ Tip

■ You can organize your .Mac Bookmarks by making the changes first in Safari and then synchronizing your bookmarks with your .Mac account.

Figure 7.18 Your new folder appears in the appropriate collection, ready for your use.

Removing Bookmarks and Folders

.Mac allows you to remove items as well as add them, a blessing for those who need to do a little pruning in an overly large collection. You can use this feature to delete either an individual bookmark or a whole folder.

To delete a .Mac Bookmarks folder or bookmark:

1. Open your .Mac Bookmarks window.

2. Navigate to the location that contains the bookmark or folder you want to delete.

3. Click the Delete button at the bottom of the window (**Figure 7.19**). The Delete button looks like a circle with a line through it.

   Delete buttons—circles with embedded white Xs—appear next to each item in the window (**Figure 7.20**).

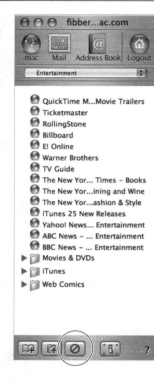

Figure 7.19 The Delete button at the bottom of the window lets you delete a bookmark or folder.

Figure 7.20 When you click the Delete button, small circles with white embedded Xs appear to the left of all visible items. These are individual Delete buttons.

Figure 7.21 When you click an item's Delete button, a message appears at the bottom of the window asking if you're sure you want to delete the item. Click Delete.

Figure 7.22 After confirming that you do indeed want to delete the selected item, the .Mac Bookmarks window reloads with the item removed.

4. Click the Delete button next to the item you want to delete.

The bottom portion of the window expands to ask if you are sure you want to delete the item (**Figure 7.21**).

5. Click Delete.

The .Mac Bookmarks window reloads with the deleted item removed (**Figure 7.22**). The next time you synchronize your bookmarks with your .Mac account, the deleted item will be removed from your Safari bookmarks.

✔ Tip

■ You can delete only one bookmark or folder at a time, so if you want to do some serious spring cleaning, you may have to repeat this process several times. You might consider making the changes in Safari instead, and then synchronizing your bookmarks.

REMOVING BOOKMARKS AND FOLDERS

Setting Bookmark Preferences

As with most other aspects of your .Mac account, you can customize how .Mac handles bookmark display and synchronization by setting your .Mac Bookmark preferences (**Figure 7.23**).

To open the .Mac Bookmarks preferences window, log in to your .Mac account and open the .Mac Bookmarks window, then click the Preferences button in the lower right corner (it's the one that looks like a light switch). This loads the .Mac Bookmarks preferences window, the settings of which you can change as follows:

◆ **Always open pages in a new browser window**—If it's not already selected, click this radio button to cause pages opened from your .Mac Bookmarks to open in a new browser window instead of your current browser window. This is the default setting.

◆ **Always open pages in the same browser window**—Select this radio button to cause pages opened from your .Mac Bookmarks to open in your current browser window.

◆ **Default folder to open**—By default, the All Collections folder is opened when you open your .Mac Bookmarks window (this simply sets your view to the top level of your bookmarks). You can, however, specify a different folder to open by default, by choosing it from the "Default folder to open" pop-up menu.

◆ **Language**—Your .Mac Bookmarks can be displayed either in English or Japanese—you choose which one from the Language pop-up menu.

◆ **Turn on .Mac Bookmarks Synchronization**—This check box lets you determine whether your .Mac Bookmarks are synchronized. This means that changes you make to your .Mac Bookmarks are reflected on computers subscribed to this .Mac account.

After you've made your changes to your .Mac Bookmarks preferences, click Save to apply them.

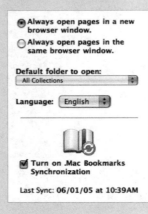

Figure 7.23 The .Mac Bookmarks preferences window lets you customize your .Mac Bookmarks experience by choosing where links open, what collection opens by default, the default language, and whether bookmarks are synchronized.

USING iCAL

iCal, Apple's free calendaring software, is included with Mac OS X 10.4 Tiger and offers some unique features to .Mac members. Anyone running Mac OS X can use iCal to keep track of calendar events, set alarms for events, and create and manage to-do lists, but .Mac members can also publish their calendars using their .Mac accounts so that anyone with a Web browser can view them. In addition, other Mac OS X users can subscribe to calendars published on .Mac using iCal, so that the subscribed calendars appear inside iCal, next to all their other calendars—and can even be automatically updated when changes occur.

In this chapter, I'll show you how to publish your calendars, view your calendars using a Web browser, subscribe to other calendars, and remove calendars.

Publishing Calendars

iCal paired with a .Mac account is a powerful combination. With it, you can publish your calendars on your .Mac account so that others can see your schedule and the events you have planned. As a side benefit, you can also view your calendars from anyplace where you have access to a Web browser.

To publish a calendar:

1. In the Applications folder, double-click the iCal icon to open the application.

   The main iCal window opens (**Figure 8.1**).

2. From the Calendars section on the left, select the calendar you want to publish.

3. From the Calendar menu, choose Publish (**Figure 8.2**).

   A sheet slides down that lets you control what information is published, as well as where it's published.

4. In the sheet, *do the following* (**Figure 8.3**):

   ▲ In the "Publish calendar as" field, type a name for your calendar. Refrain from using non-alphanumeric characters (such as spaces), or you'll have to use the URL-safe versions of those characters. For example, a calendar titled My Calendar becomes My%20Calendar when listed in a URL. This is simply because URLs can't have spaces, so the space in the calendar name is encoded as %20. Bottom line: Avoid non-alphanumeric characters when publishing a calendar.

   ▲ From the "Publish on" pop-up menu, choose .Mac, if it's not already selected.

   ▲ If you want calendar information updated as it's changed in iCal, check the "Publish changes automatically" check box.

Figure 8.1 iCal's main interface is pretty simple—familiar visual calendar with all scheduled events on the right, and individual calendars listed on the left. Select a calendar in the list to prepare to publish it.

Figure 8.2 When you choose Publish from the Calendar menu, the calendar publishing sheet allows you to name the calendar, specify where it will be published, and indicate what content is published.

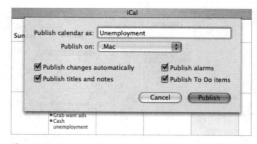

Figure 8.3 Once you've customized how your calendar will be published, click Publish.

Figure 8.4 After you've published a calendar, the Calendar Published dialog appears, giving you several options on what to do next. You can visit the calendar's page, send an e-mail announcing the page, or simply dismiss the dialog by clicking OK.

Figure 8.5 If you click the Visit Page button after publishing a calendar, the calendar opens in your Web browser.

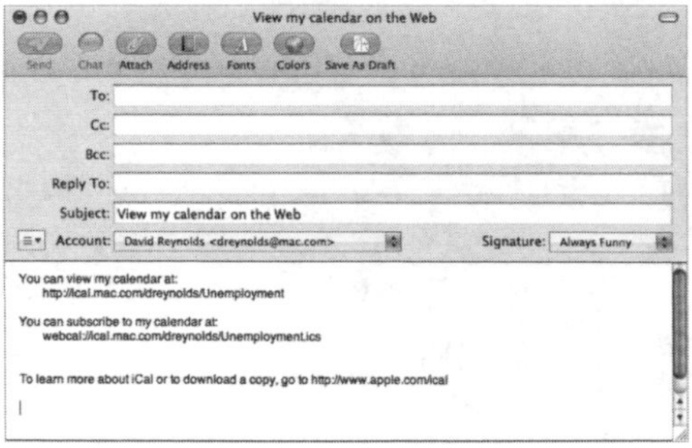

Figure 8.6 If you click the Send Mail button after publishing a calendar, an e-mail message is automatically generated in your e-mail client, complete with the details concerning your new calendar.

▲ To publish the titles and notes for the calendar's events, check the "Publish titles and notes" check box.

▲ To publish alarms associated with the selected calendar, check the "Publish alarms" check box.

▲ To publish To Do items associated with the calendar, check the "Publish To Do items" check box.

5. Click Publish.

The calendar is uploaded to your .Mac account, and the Calendar Published dialog opens (**Figure 8.4**). This dialog provides the URL for subscribing to the calendar as well as the URL for viewing the calendar using a Web browser.

6. To open the calendar in your Web browser, click the Visit Page button (**Figure 8.5**).

or

To generate an e-mail message announcing the calendar in your default e-mail client, click the Send Mail button (**Figure 8.6**).

or

To dismiss the dialog, click OK.

✔ Tips

■ If you have private calendars that you want to keep secure, don't publish them on your .Mac account where anyone with a Web browser who knows the URLs can view them.

■ You can also publish calendars to private servers with iCal. Choose Calendar > Publish. In the sheet that slides down, choose "a Private Server" from the "Publish on" pop-up menu. This is useful if you want to keep your calendars private, such as with an intranet. Remember—.Mac calendars are neither private nor secure.

To unpublish a calendar:

1. In the Applications folder, double-click the iCal icon to open the application.

The main iCal window opens; in the Calendars section on the left, published calendars have a small mark to the right of their names indicating that they have been published (**Figure 8.7**).

2. In the Calendars section, select the calendar you want to unpublish.

3. From the Calendar menu, choose Unpublish (**Figure 8.8**).

A dialog appears, asking you to confirm that you want to unpublish the calendar (**Figure 8.9**).

4. Click Unpublish.

The calendar is no longer published on your .Mac account, and the published mark disappears (**Figure 8.10**).

Figure 8.7 Calendars that you've published show a small marker to the right of their names that looks like waves emanating from a point.

Figure 8.8 To unpublish a calendar, select the calendar and then choose Unpublish from the Calendar menu.

Figure 8.9 Before you can unpublish a calendar, iCal first asks if you're sure you want to do that. Click Unpublish.

Figure 8.10 After you've unpublished a calendar, the publish marker no longer appears to the right of its name in the Calendars column.

Removing an Orphaned Calendar

It's important to note that if you delete an iCal calendar without unpublishing it (say you forget to unpublish it before deleting it), you won't be able to make changes to it. Others, however, *will* still be able to subscribe to the last published version of that calendar.

To get rid of one of these orphaned calendars, do the following:

1. Create a new calendar in iCal with the same name as the published calendar you deleted.

2. Publish the new calendar with the same name as your old calendar. This will replace the existing calendar in your .Mac account.

3. Unpublish the newly created calendar as described in "To unpublish a calendar."

4. Delete the newly created calendar from iCal.

The orphaned calendar will be replaced with the newly created faux calendar when you publish it (just as an empty file with the same name replaces a large one). Then, when you unpublish it, the faux calendar comes off of .Mac, leaving it clean.

Subscribing to Calendars

You can use iCal to subscribe to a calendar that someone else (or you, if you like) has published to a .Mac membership. This imports the calendar into your copy of iCal, so that you can view that calendar without opening a Web browser. You can customize your subscription by updating the subscription on a regular basis, as well as removing alarms and To Do items.

To subscribe to a calendar:

1. In the Applications folder, double-click the iCal icon to open the application.

   The main iCal window opens.

2. From the Calendar menu, choose Subscribe (Command-Option-S) (**Figure 8.11**).

   The "Subscribe to" sheet slides down.

3. In the "Subscribe to" field, type the URL of the calendar you're subscribing to (**Figure 8.12**).

   The URL should begin with *webcal://*.

4. Click Subscribe.

   The calendar is downloaded, and the "Subscribing to" sheet appears, asking you to customize the subscription.

5. In the "Subscribing to" sheet, *do the following* (**Figure 8.13**):

   ▲ In the Title field, type a title for the calendar (one is supplied for you).

   ▲ If you want to have your calendar automatically updated, check the Refresh check box.

   ▲ From the Refresh pop-up menu, choose a frequency for the updates. Your choices are "every 15 minutes," "every hour," "every day," and "every week."

Figure 8.11 To subscribe to an iCal calendar, choose Subscribe from the Calendar menu.

Figure 8.12 To subscribe to an iCal calendar, enter its URL in the "Subscribe to" field. The URL should begin with *webcal://*.

Figure 8.13 In the "Subscribing to" sheet, you can give the calendar a name, set how often it's checked for new information, and set whether alarms and To Do items are also subscribed to by checking the appropriate boxes.

Figure 8.14 Once you've subscribed to a calendar, it appears in the Calendars section of your iCal page.

Figure 8.15 Before you can unsubscribe from a calendar—that is, delete it from your list—iCal asks if you're sure this is something you want to do. Click Delete to proceed.

Figure 8.16 After you've removed a calendar to which you've subscribed, it no longer shows up in the Calendars section.

▲ To remove all alarms from the calendar, check the "Remove alarms" box.

▲ To remove To Do items from the calendar, check the "Remove To Do items" check box.

6. Click OK.

The calendar is added to the bottom of iCal's Calendars column on the left side of the window (**Figure 8.14**).

✔ Tips

■ To find out the URL of a calendar, you can do the following: combine webcal://ical.mac.com/ with the .Mac member name, a slash, the calendar's published name, and finally .ics. So, the URL for a .Mac member named bigbill who has published a calendar named Parties would look like webcal://ical.mac.com/bigbill/Parties.ics. Or, you could just ask bigbill, who would be happy to give you his Parties calendar URL.

■ You can find more calendars to subscribe to at www.apple.com/macosx/features/ical/library and www.icalshare.com.

To unsubscribe from a calendar:

1. In the Applications folder, double-click the iCal icon to open the application.

The main iCal window opens.

2. From the Calendars section of the window on the left, select the calendar you want to unsubscribe from.

3. Press the Delete key.

A dialog pops up, asking if you're sure you want to remove the calendar (**Figure 8.15**).

4. Click Delete.

You are unsubscribed from the calendar, and it is removed from your iCal calendar (**Figure 8.16**).

Viewing Calendars Online

When you publish a calendar from iCal on your .Mac account, you can view it using a Web browser. The corollary to this is that you can view *any* published iCal calendar using a Web browser, provided you know the name of the calendar and the member name of the person publishing it.

To view an iCal calendar online:

1. Open your Web browser.

2. In the location field, enter http://ical. mac.com/*membername*/*calendarname* and press Return—replacing *member-name* with the .Mac member name of the person publishing the iCal calendar and replacing *calendarname* with the name of the calendar you want to view.

   The calendar opens in your Web browser, showing the Week view by default.

3. To view the calendar one day at a time, click the Day button (**Figure 8.17**).

   The calendar switches to Day view (**Figure 8.18**).

Figure 8.17 Click the Day button to change the calendar to the Day view.

Figure 8.18 A calendar's Day view focuses on events for a single day—letting you see how things are supposed to play out, minute by minute.

Figure 8.19 A calendar's Month view displays an entire month at a time, with a summary of the month's scheduled events at the bottom.

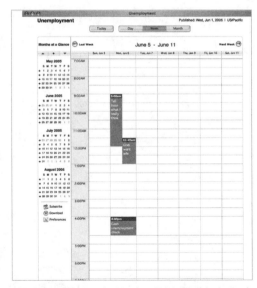

Figure 8.20 The Week view (a calendar's default view) shows the week at a glance, also providing a time frame for each event—a nice cross between the Day and Month views.

4. To view the calendar one month at a time, click the Month button.

The calendar switches to Month view (**Figure 8.19**).

5. To view today's calendar, click the Today button.

The calendar for the day you're working in opens.

6. To view the calendar one week at a time, click the Week button.

The calendar switches to Week view (**Figure 8.20**).

To subscribe to a calendar online:

1. Open your Web browser.

2. In the location field, enter http://ical. mac.com/*membername*/*calendarname* and press Return—replacing *member-name* with the .Mac member name of the person publishing the iCal calendar and replacing *calendarname* with the name of the calendar you want to view.

   The calendar opens in your Web browser.

3. In the lower left column, click the Subscribe button (**Figure 8.21**).

   iCal opens and presents you with the "Subscribe to" sheet, with the URL filled in automatically (**Figure 8.22**).

4. Click Subscribe.

   The subscribed calendar appears in iCal.

Figure 8.21 Click the Subscribe button to launch iCal and subscribe to the calendar you're viewing in your Web browser.

Figure 8.22 After you click Subscribe, the "Subscribe to" sheet slides down, with the URL for the calendar you were just viewing filled in. To subscribe, click the Subscribe button.

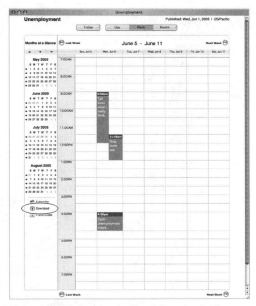

Figure 8.23 To download a file of the calendar (in a format that can be read by some other calendaring programs, such as Microsoft Entourage), click the Download link.

Figure 8.24 When you click a calendar event, a window pops up with more information about that event, showing its title, start date, and end date.

Figure 8.25 To browse through a calendar, click the Last and Next buttons at the top of the calendar's browser window.

To download a calendar:

1. Open a calendar in a Web browser.

2. In the lower left column, click the Download button (**Figure 8.23**).

   A calendar file downloads to the folder where files are normally downloaded. You can import this calendar file into calendaring programs that don't support subscriptions, such as Microsoft Entourage.

✔ Tips

- To import a calendar file into another program, typically you can either drop the calendar file on the program's icon, or import the file through the program's import function.

- To view more information about a calendar event, click it in the browser window.

  A window pops up with more information about the event (**Figure 8.24**).

- You can browse through a calendar by clicking the Last and Next buttons at the top or bottom of the calendar's browser window (**Figure 8.25**).

- To view an individual day, click it in the Months at a Glance sidebar. The day will load in the browser window.

VIEWING CALENDARS ONLINE

Setting Calendar Preferences

You can set a calendar's viewing preferences by clicking the Preferences button in the lower left column of the calendar's Web page (**Figure 8.26**). When this page opens (**Figure 8.27**), you can alter the following settings:

◆ **Choose a language**—From the "Choose a language" pop-up menu, choose which of 15 languages the calendar is displayed in.

◆ **Choose whether the event list is displayed**—From the "Event list" pop-up menu, choose On or Off to set whether the event list appears at the bottom of the calendar in Month view.

◆ **Choose a default calendar view**—From the "Default calendar" pop-up menu, select Daily, Weekly, or Monthly to set which view is the default.

◆ **Choose the day the week starts on**—From the "Start week on" pop-up menu, choose a day of the week on which you want calendars to start. By default, this is set to Sunday, but no one's stopping you from setting it to Thursday, if you like.

◆ **Choose how the time is displayed**—From the "Time display" pop-up menu, choose whether calendars are displayed using a 12 Hour or 24 Hour clock.

Once you've made your selections, click the Apply button in the lower right corner to save your changes.

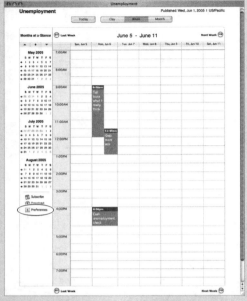

Figure 8.26 Click the Preferences button to load the preferences for that Web calendar.

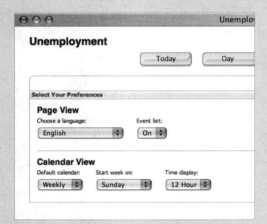

Figure 8.27 On the calendar preferences page, you can change some settings that govern how the calendar behaves—such as the language it's displayed in, whether the event list is shown, and what the default calendar view looks like.

USING BACKUP

One of the many perks of having a .Mac account is that you get a copy of Apple's file-backup program, named, appropriately, Backup. With it, you can set up your system to automatically copy important files to your iDisk, to a network volume, or to another hard drive, or even burn them to CD or DVD—or do some combination of the above.

The information on your computer—all of your e-mail messages, letters, digital photos, everything—is there because of incredibly complex electronic devices and equally complex hardware that keep everything in order. But, inevitably, something happens to one of those systems, and some or all of that precious data evaporates, never to be seen again. It's personally happened to me twice.

Backup offers hope. Properly used, it's a great way to ensure that you don't lose any valuable data. Once you've set up your backup scheme, Backup does the heavy lifting for you. It copies the latest versions of your files, so that if something happens to your local copy, you can easily restore your lost files. In this chapter, I'll show you how to install and set up Backup to protect your data.

Installing Backup

Backup comes in two flavors: version 2 for Mac OS X 10.2.6 or later, and version 1.1 for Mac OS X 10.1. Sorry, Mac OS 9 users—you're out of luck on this one. In order to use Backup, you need a currently active .Mac account—either a full account for all features or a trial account for iDisk-only backup. Be sure your .Mac member name and password are entered in the .Mac section of System Preferences.

Backup's user interface is pretty basic—it asks where you want your backup files stored and shows you how much space is available there. It also lets you select what groups of files to back up, as well as add items, refresh your list, schedule backups, and eject the medium to which you're backing up all your files.

But first you must download and install the Backup software.

To download and install Backup:

1. Using a Web browser, log in to your .Mac account (**Figure 9.1**).

   The main .Mac Web page loads.

2. On the left side of the page, click Backup (**Figure 9.2**).

   The Backup 2 page loads.

Figure 9.1 Before you can download the Backup software, you'll need to log in to your .Mac account by entering your .Mac member name and password.

Figure 9.2 Click the Backup link from the main page to go to the Backup download and information page.

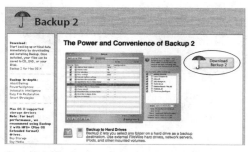

Figure 9.3 The Backup page contains links to download the Backup software, as well as to pages that provide in-depth information on the program.

Figure 9.4 The Backup download page has download links for two versions of Backup: Backup 1 and Backup 2. Click the download link for the version appropriate to your operating system.

Figure 9.5 The Backup disc image contains the installer package for Backup. Double-click its icon to launch the installer.

3. In the upper right corner of the page, click Download Backup 2 (**Figure 9.3**).

The main Backup download page loads. Here, you're presented with a choice of which version of Backup to download—1.1 or 2.

4. If you're using Mac OS X 10.1, click the link to download Backup 1.1. If you're using Mac OS X 10.2.6 or later, click the link to download Backup 2 (**Figure 9.4**).

Backup is downloaded to your hard drive in the location to which you normally download files.

5. Once the disk-image file downloads to your hard drive, mount it by double-clicking it (if it's not automatically mounted).

The disk image mounts (**Figure 9.5**).

(continues on next page)

INSTALLING BACKUP

6. Open the Backup disk image, and then double-click the Backup.pkg icon to launch the Backup installer.

The Welcome pane appears (**Figure 9.6**).

7. Click Continue.

The Important Information pane opens, which contains valuable information about installing and using Backup (**Figure 9.7**).

8. Click Continue.

The Backup Software License Agreement pane loads (**Figure 9.8**).

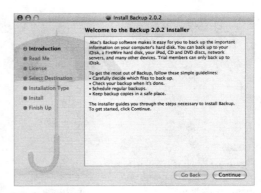

Figure 9.6 The Backup installer's Welcome pane gives you an overview of Backup. Click Continue to move on to the next step.

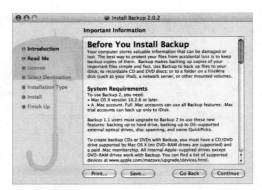

Figure 9.7 The Important Information pane contains valuable information about how to install and use Backup. Read it and click Continue.

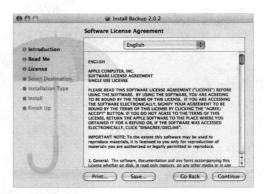

Figure 9.8 The Backup Software License Agreement is a legal document—it's worth reading this to see what you're agreeing to. Click Continue to move on.

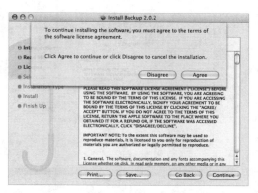

Figure 9.9 To continue with the installation, you must click the Agree button in the Software License Agreement pane.

Figure 9.10 The Select a Destination pane lists all valid locations for a Backup installation. Select the one you want (usually your main hard drive) and click Continue.

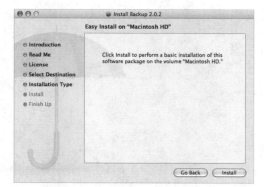

Figure 9.11 On the Installation Type pane, there isn't much to do, since Backup doesn't have any installation options. Click Install.

9. Click Continue.

A sheet slides down, noting that in order to continue to install Backup, you must agree to the terms of the license agreement (**Figure 9.9**).

10. Click Agree.

The Select a Destination pane loads; it lists all available locations where you can install Backup (**Figure 9.10**).

11. Select a destination volume and click Continue.

The Installation Type pane loads (**Figure 9.11**).

(continues on next page)

12. Click Install.

The Authenticate pane loads (**Figure 9.12**).

13. Type your system password and click OK.

The installer installs Backup in the Applications folder of your hard drive and does some other housekeeping (**Figure 9.13**). When it's finished, a message appears, noting that Backup has finished installing.

14. Click Close (**Figure 9.14**).

Backup is now installed in your Applications folder.

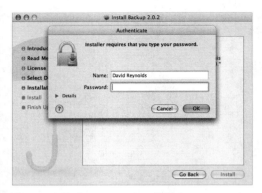

Figure 9.12 Before you can install Backup, you must type in your administrator password and click OK.

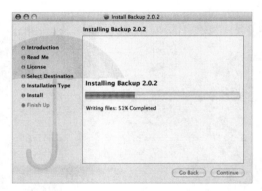

Figure 9.13 The Backup installer writes the necessary files to your hard drive and performs some other housekeeping.

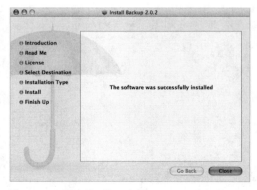

Figure 9.14 Click the Close button to complete the installation of Backup 2.

Setting Up a Backup

The general process of setting up Backup to protect your important data is fairly easy, although there are a number of choices to be made during the process—mostly revolving around where you want your backups to be made.

You have three choices:

◆ Back up to iDisk—This creates a backup on your iDisk over your Internet connection. Choose this option if you have a high-speed Internet connection, and be sure to limit the number of files you back up, or you'll overwhelm your iDisk.

◆ Back up to CD/DVD—This creates a backup on recordable CDs or DVDs using your Mac's CD or DVD burner. Choose this option to create durable backups of your data, but remember—you'll have to be by your Mac during the backup to provide it with blank discs.

◆ Back up to Drive—This creates a backup on another hard drive or network volume. Choose this option to back up your important data to another hard drive or network volume.

When you fire up Backup for the first time, you'll be presented with its default setup. Although Backup *can* be set up to back up just about any files to just about any location on a schedule, it's not set up that way when you launch it. It's your job to customize these settings to suit your needs. Doing so is a three-step process: choosing where you want the files to be backed up, selecting which files are to be backed up, and setting up a schedule of when backups occur.

Backup Strategy

A good backup strategy involves making two or more backups, preferably stored in two or more locations. That way, if your main computer and one of your backups is destroyed, you'll have a second copy. Sure, it sounds redundant, but here's an example—you've made a backup of your computer to DVD, and you've stored it in your basement. Then you have a house fire that starts in your basement and consumes not only your backup, but your computer, too. Do yourself a favor—make two or more backups and put them in different physical locations, especially for important things such as financial data.

To back up to iDisk:

1. In the Applications folder, double-click the Backup icon to launch the software.

   Backup checks for an iDisk server as it launches. If this is the first time you've launched Backup, you may receive a message saying that BackupHelper wants permission to access your keychain (**Figure 9.15**). This is OK. If you've already launched Backup, go to Step 3.

2. Click Always Allow.

   If this is the first time you've launched Backup, a dialog appears, thanking you for joining .Mac (**Figure 9.16**).

3. Click OK.

   Backup displays its main window (**Figure 9.17**).

Figure 9.15 If this is the first time you've launched Backup, you may be asked for access to your keychain. This is OK; click Always Allow.

Figure 9.16 If this is the first time you've launched Backup, it thanks you for joining and provides some additional information. Click OK.

Figure 9.17 The main Backup window is a pretty simple affair. It asks where files should be backed up; it provides a graphical representation of how much space is available on your iDisk; it lists the items to be backed up; it provides some information on scheduling and file size; and it has some basic controls, including a Backup Now button.

Figure 9.18 The Backup pop-up menu offers three backup choices: Back up to iDisk, Back up to CD/DVD, and Back up to Drive. You need to choose one of them to create a backup.

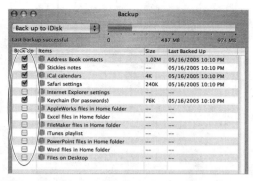

Figure 9.19 When you check the boxes to the left of the items you want to have backed up, Backup will scan your hard drive for those items and automatically include them.

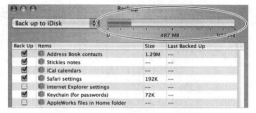

Figure 9.20 When backing up files to your iDisk, check the gauge at the top to ensure that you have enough space available for the files you've selected in the Back Up column.

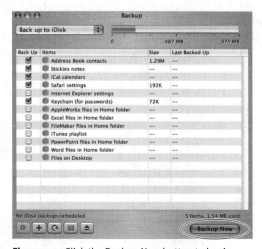

Figure 9.21 Click the Backup Now button to begin your backup.

4. From the pop-up menu in the upper left corner, choose Back up to iDisk (**Figure 9.18**).

5. In the Back Up column of the main window, check the boxes to the left of the items that you want to back up (**Figure 9.19**).

6. At the top of the window, check the available-space gauge to ensure that you have enough space to copy the selected items. This gauge appears when you select Back up to iDisk in step 4 (**Figure 9.20**).

7. In the lower right corner of the window, click the Backup Now button (**Figure 9.21**).

Backup scans for the files to be saved and goes straight to work creating your backup in the location you've specified. You'll see a progress bar as items are copied to the location you set in step 4.

✔ Tip

- When backing up files to your iDisk, you'll need to have your .Mac member name and password entered in the .Mac system preferences, and you'll have to have Internet access (which makes sense when you think about it). A backup can potentially take up gigabytes of space, so when backing up to your iDisk, remember that you'll need to make the backup small enough to fit on your iDisk.

To back up to a CD or DVD:

1. Open Backup.

If this is the first time you've launched Backup, you may receive a message saying that BackupHelper wants permission to access your keychain (see Figure 9.15). This is OK. If you've already launched Backup, go to step 3.

2. Click Always Allow.

If this is the first time you've launched Backup, a dialog appears, thanking you for joining .Mac (see Figure 9.16).

3. Click OK.

Backup displays its main window.

4. From the pop-up menu in the upper left corner, choose Back up to CD/DVD (**Figure 9.22**).

5. In the Back Up column of the main window, check the boxes to the left of the items that you want to back up (**Figure 9.23**).

6. In the lower right corner of the window, click the Backup Now button.

A dialog pops up, asking you to name your backup.

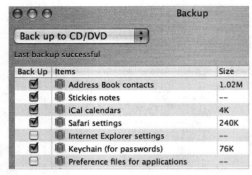

Figure 9.22 Choose Back up to CD/DVD from the Backup pop-up menu to back up items to optical discs.

Figure 9.23 When you check the boxes to the left of the items you want to have backed up, Backup will scan your hard drive for those items and automatically include them.

Figure 9.24 Before backing up to CD/DVD media, Backup requires you to name your backup. It provides a good one, though—the current date and time. If you like this name, or after you've typed in a name of your own, click Begin Backup.

Figure 9.25 To continue the backup process, insert a CD and click Burn when the button becomes activated.

Figure 9.26 Click the Burn button to burn the backup to CD or DVD.

Figure 9.27 After you click the Burn button, Backup goes to work gathering files and burning them to CD or DVD.

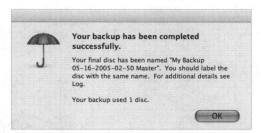

Figure 9.28 When finished, Backup tells you whether the backup process was successful, what to label the disc, and how many discs the process used.

7. In the "Name your backup" field, type a name for your backup, and then click Begin Backup (**Figure 9.24**).

   Backup asks you to insert a disc (**Figure 9.25**).

8. Insert a disc.

   The Burn button is activated.

9. Click Burn (**Figure 9.26**).

   Backup burns the files to the disc that you inserted (**Figure 9.27**). Depending on the size of the backup, you may need to insert more than one disc when asked. When finished with the process, Backup provides a short summary dialog, giving you the name that you should use to label the CD or DVD, and noting how many discs the backup used (**Figure 9.28**).

10. Click OK to finish.

✔ Tips

- When you back up your data to CDs or DVDs, Backup tells you in advance how many blank disks you'll need to do the job.

- Backup allows backing up to CDs and DVDs only if your Mac has a Mac OS X–supported optical drive—there's a complete list at Mac OS X Storage Device Support (www.apple.com/macosx/upgrade/storage.html).

To back up to a drive:

1. Open Backup.

   If this is the first time you've launched Backup, you may receive a message saying that BackupHelper wants permission to access your keychain (see Figure 9.15). This is OK. If you've already launched Backup, go to step 3.

2. Click Always Allow.

   If this is the first time you've launched Backup, a dialog appears, thanking you for joining .Mac (see Figure 9.16).

3. Click OK.

   Backup displays its main window.

4. From the pop-up menu in the upper left corner, choose Back up to Drive (**Figure 9.29**).

5. At the top of the window, click the Set button (**Figure 9.30**).

6. In the "Set a backup location" sheet that drops down, click Create (**Figure 9.31**).

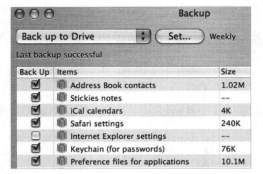

Figure 9.29 Select Back up to Drive from the Backup pop-up menu to back up items to hard drives or network volumes.

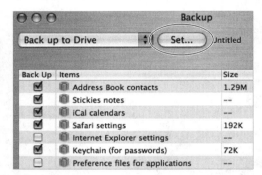

Figure 9.30 Click the Set button to set a location on a drive for your backup.

Figure 9.31 Click Create to create a new backup file and set a location in which backups will take place.

Figure 9.32 In the file browser, navigate to the location you want to use for your backup, give it a name in the Save As field, and click Create. We're calling this backup "Weekly" to indicate how often we'll use it for a backup, but you can name it practically anything.

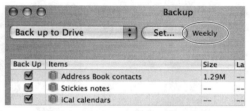

Figure 9.33 The main Backup window has your new backup listed at the top. Here, it's named Weekly, but it could be named anything—even "Spike MacRashton."

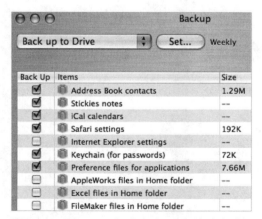

Figure 9.34 When you check the boxes to the left of the items you want to have backed up, Backup will scan your hard drive for those items and automatically include them.

7. In the file browser window that rolls down, navigate to the location you want to use for the backup, type a name for your backup in the Save As field, and click Create (**Figure 9.32**).

Backup displays its main window with the new location represented in the top portion of the window, just to the right of the Set button (**Figure 9.33**).

8. In the Back Up column, check the boxes of the items that you want to back up (**Figure 9.34**).

(continues on next page)

9. In the lower right corner of the window, click the Backup Now button (**Figure 9.35**).

Backup scans for the files to be saved and goes straight to work creating your backup in the location you've specified. You'll see a progress bar as items are copied to the location you set in Step 4.

✔ Tip

■ Although you can back up your files to the same hard drive, it's not a very good idea. What happens if your drive crashes? You lose your originals and your backup, that's what.

Figure 9.35 Click the Backup Now button to begin your backup.

Using QuickPicks

Backup comes prepopulated with a series of items (called QuickPicks) that make it easy to automate backups. These QuickPicks back up information that's likely to be important—especially information of which you may not know the location (think back to the last time you knew where your Adobe Photoshop preferences or Actions Palette files are stored).

The selection of QuickPicks varies, depending on the backup location you've selected (after all, no one can copy respectable iPhoto and iTunes libraries to an iDisk, the combination of which would be many gigabytes more than an iDisk can hold).

To take advantage of these QuickPicks, simply check the boxes next to the ones you want to use. Backup will do any necessary configuration for you (such as scanning for the files to be included), and the items will be included in the backup.

(continues on next page)

These QuickPicks cover the following (**Figure 9.36**):

◆ **Address Book contacts**—Backs up the contact information you have stored in Address Book.

◆ **Stickies notes**—If you use Stickies, this QuickPick will back up your notes.

◆ **iCal calendars**—Creates a copy of your iCal calendar information.

◆ **Safari settings**—Backs up your Safari settings and bookmarks, as well as any cache files (this can make your Safari backup larger than it might otherwise be).

◆ **Internet Explorer settings**—Backs up your Microsoft Internet Explorer bookmarks and settings.

◆ **Keychain (for passwords)**—Makes a copy of passwords that you've entered in the Keychain application.

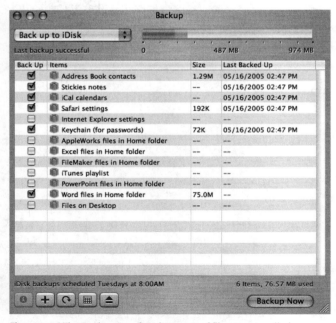

Figure 9.36 The Backup interface has a set of file groups, called QuickPicks, that you can use to quickly create a backup.

◆ **Preferences** (not available for iDisk backups)—Backs up the preference files for all of your applications. This one's a *huge* deal—it catches all of those files that keep your Mac's applications acting the way you expect, and those same files are quite difficult to find on your hard drive otherwise.

◆ **AppleWorks files in Home folder**—Scans all files in your home directory and makes a backup of all AppleWorks files.

◆ **Excel files in Home folder**—Scans all files in your home directory and makes a backup of all Microsoft Excel files.

◆ **FileMaker files in Home folder**—Scans all files in your home directory and makes a backup of all FileMaker databases.

◆ **iPhoto library**—Copies your iPhoto digital photography. Since these backups can be really large, this option isn't available for iDisk backups.

◆ **iTunes library**—Copies your iTunes music library. Again, since these can be really large backups, this option isn't available for iDisk backups.

◆ **iTunes playlist**—Makes a copy of any iTunes playlists. This option is only available for iDisk backups.

◆ **iTunes purchases**—Makes a copy of any iTunes purchased music. This option is not available for iDisk backups.

◆ **PowerPoint files in Home folder**—Scans all files in your home directory and makes a backup of all Microsoft PowerPoint files.

◆ **Word files in Home folder**—Scans all files in your home directory and makes a backup of all Microsoft Word files.

◆ **Files on Desktop**—Makes a copy of all the files you keep on your Desktop.

Adding File Groups

Although you can perform a perfectly good backup using just QuickPicks, you can also choose your own collections of files and folders to back up.

To add a file group:

1. Open Backup.

Backup displays its main window.

2. *Do one of the following:*

▲ In the Finder, select the files you want to back up and drag them into the Backup window (**Figure 9.37**).

▲ In the lower left corner of the main Backup window, click the Plus (+) button (**Figure 9.38**) to bring up a file-browser window. Navigate to the folder that you want to back up and click Choose (**Figure 9.39**).

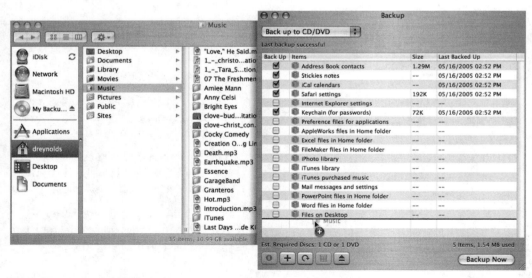

Figure 9.37 Drag the files or folders (or any combination of them) into the Backup window to add them as QuickPicks.

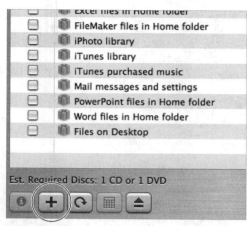

Figure 9.38 Click the Plus (+) button to open a file browser that allows you to choose files or folders to include in a backup group.

The items you dragged into the window appear as files and folders below the QuickPicks in the list. These files and folders have checked boxes next to them, indicating that they will be backed up during the next backup operation (**Figure 9.40**).

✔ Tip

■ You can drag files and folders from any Finder window, including a Search Results window. To create a backup list of files you search for, perform a search and then drag the items you want to back up from the Search Results window into the Backup window.

Figure 9.39 Once you've navigated to the file or folder you want to include in a file group, click Choose.

Figure 9.40 The file or folder you choose appears at the bottom of the window with its box checked, ready to be included during the next backup.

To remove a file group:

1. Open Backup.

   Backup displays its main window.

2. Select the file or folder you want to remove while pressing the Control key.

   A contextual menu appears under the pointer with one choice—Delete.

3. Choose Delete from the menu (**Figure 9.41**).

   The item is deleted from the list of files to be backed up.

✔ Tips

- You can also delete an item by selecting it in the window and pressing Delete.

- If you've got a two-button mouse, you can also remove an item from the list of QuickPicks and folders by simply right-clicking it. If you delete a standard QuickPick and later decide you want that QuickPick back, simply choose Edit > Restore All QuickPicks.

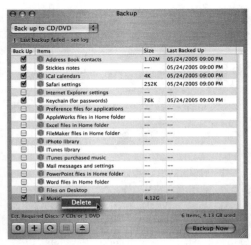

Figure 9.41 Choosing Delete from the contextual menu brought up by Control-clicking an item deletes the item from the QuickPick list.

Getting More Backup Information

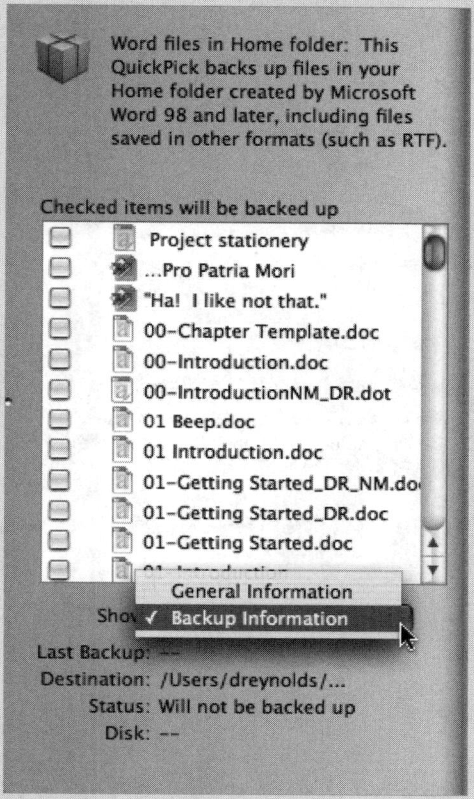

Word files in Home folder: This QuickPick backs up files in your Home folder created by Microsoft Word 98 and later, including files saved in other formats (such as RTF).

Checked items will be backed up

- Project stationery
- ...Pro Patria Mori
- "Ha! I like not that."
- 00–Chapter Template.doc
- 00–Introduction.doc
- 00–IntroductionNM_DR.dot
- 01 Beep.doc
- 01 Introduction.doc
- 01–Getting Started_DR_NM.do
- 01–Getting Started_DR.doc
- 01–Getting Started.doc

General Information
Sho ✓ Backup Information

Last Backup: --
Destination: /Users/dreynolds/...
Status: Will not be backed up
Disk: --

Figure 9.42 The information drawer shows more information on the files in a given QuickPick, allowing you to find out more about individual files, including when they were backed up. Checking boxes to the left of items in the information drawer for some QuickPicks allows you to select individual items to be backed up.

If you want to know what an item actually backs up (either a QuickPick or another folder), select the item in the list and then click the Information button (the one with the lowercase "i" inside a circle, in the lower-left corner of the main Backup window), or just double-click the item. A sidebar drawer opens, revealing more information about what files will be backed up and allowing you to control which files in a group are copied (**Figure 9.42**).

To choose whether a file or folder in the selected item will be backed up, simply make sure the box next to it is checked.

From the Show pop-up menu at the bottom of the sidebar, you can select whether General Information (such as the kind, size, and last-modified date) or Backup Information (such as time of last backup) appears below the file list.

In some cases (such as with application files—Word files, PowerPoint files, and the like), you can check the boxes to the left of the individual items to indicate whether those items will be backed up, which lets you further customize QuickPicks and your own file groups.

ADDING FILE GROUPS

Scheduling Backups

Backup's real power lies in its ability to take you out of the equation. By setting up backups on a schedule, you ensure that backups happen at a time that's convenient (such as at night), and that they actually happen.

To set up a Backup schedule:

1. Open Backup and set up a backup.

2. In the lower left corner of the window, click the Schedule button (**Figure 9.43**). This button is activated only if you've chosen to back up to your iDisk or drive. You cannot schedule automatic backups to a CD or DVD.

   The Schedule Backups sheet slides down (**Figure 9.44**).

3. *Do the following:*

   ▲ Click the Never, Daily, or Weekly radio button to set the frequency of the scheduled backup.

   ▲ From the Time of Day pop-up menus, choose the time at which you want the backup to happen (these menus will not be activated unless you click the Daily or Weekly radio button).

   ▲ From the Day of Week pop-up menu, choose the day of the week on which you want the backup to happen (this menu will not be activated unless you click the Weekly radio button).

Figure 9.43 Click the Schedule button (the one that looks like a calendar) to open the schedule sheet.

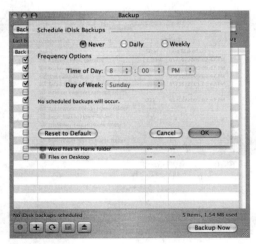

Figure 9.44 The Schedule sheet allows you to choose when backups occur.

4. Click OK.

Your backup is now scheduled. For a scheduled backup to happen, be sure your Mac is on and that you are logged in at the time when the backup is supposed to happen—otherwise, the backup won't take place. Your backup's schedule will now appear at the bottom of the window, along with the size of the backup and number of items to be backed up (**Figure 9.45**).

✔ Tips

■ The Schedule button is available only for iDisk and drive backups—CD/DVD backups can't be scheduled because they need you to be there to change discs.

■ You can set up two backups—one to your iDisk and one to a drive—that use two different schedules. Why? A good use for this is to schedule a daily backup of your most critical files to your iDisk, and a weekly backup of important (but not quite so critical) files to a drive. That way, you're sure that your most important stuff gets taken care of on a daily basis and is safe on your iDisk, without taking up the room that a more complete backup can take. The larger, weekly backup goes to a drive.

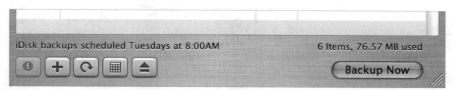

iDisk backups scheduled Tuesdays at 8:00AM   6 Items, 76.57 MB used

Backup Now

Figure 9.45 Once you've scheduled a backup, basic information about that scheduled backup appears in the main Backup window.

To turn off a Backup schedule:

1. Open Backup.

2. Click the Schedule button (**Figure 9.46**).
The schedule sheet slides down
(**Figure 9.47**).

3. Click the Never radio button to select it
(**Figure 9.48**).

4. Click OK.
Your scheduled backup has been
turned off.

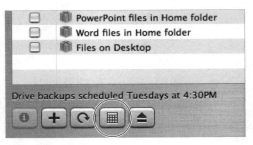

Figure 9.46 Click the Schedule button (the one that looks like a calendar) to open the schedule sheet.

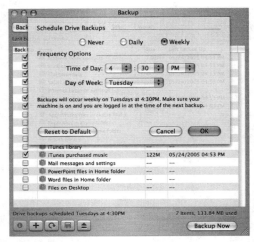

Figure 9.47 The schedule sheet allows you to choose when backups occur. It also allows you to turn off backups.

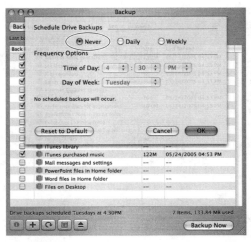

Figure 9.48 Click the Never radio button to turn off a scheduled backup.

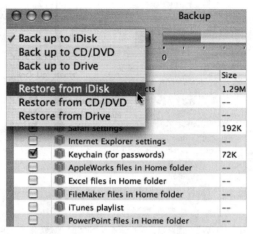

Figure 9.49 Choose the location from which you'll be restoring files from backup—iDisk, a CD/DVD, or a drive.

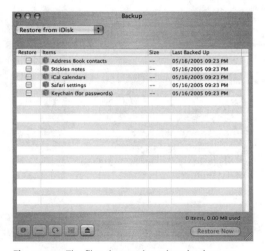

Figure 9.50 The files that are in a given backup are listed in the Restore pane.

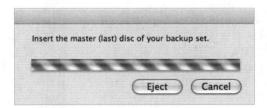

Figure 9.51 If you're restoring files from a CD or DVD backup, you will be asked to insert the master disc from the backup set. Insert the disc to continue.

Restoring Files

With luck, you won't ever *have* to restore files from a backup that you've made, but you shouldn't count on it. After all, there would be no point in creating backups if you couldn't restore your data from them.

To restore files from a backup:

1. Ensure that the media that contain your backup files are available to you. This includes CDs or DVDs, FireWire or USB hard drives, network volumes, or Internet access if you've backed up to your iDisk.

2. Open Backup.
   Backup's main window is displayed.

3. In the pop-up menu in the upper left corner, choose the source from which you want to restore your backup files (**Figure 9.49**). Your choices are Restore from iDisk, Restore from CD/DVD, and Restore from Drive.

   The Backup window lists the files that are available to be restored (**Figure 9.50**). If you're restoring files from a CD or DVD, a dialog opens, asking you to insert the appropriate CD or DVD (**Figure 9.51**).

4. If prompted, insert the master disc of your backup CD or DVD set.

5. In the list of available files, check the boxes next to the items you want to restore.

(continues on next page)

6. Click the Restore Now button (**Figure 9.52**).

If the restoration will cause a file to be overwritten, you'll be notified and asked whether you want to overwrite existing files (**Figure 9.53**).

7. Click Replace to replace the existing items with copies from the backup; click Skip to skip the replacement for that file.

Backup restores the selected files from the location to which they were backed up (**Figure 9.54**).

✔ Tips

■ If you want to restore only selected files from within an item, show the item's information by selecting it and clicking the information icon (marked with an I) in the lower right corner, or double-click the item. Then, check just the files you want to restore.

■ It's a good idea to practice restoring files from a backup. That way, if bad things happen, you can quickly restore the needed files from the backup.

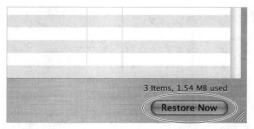

Figure 9.52 Click the Restore Now button to restore the checked items from your backup.

Figure 9.53 If you're replacing existing files with files from a backup (even ones with cryptic names, such as this one), Backup warns you and gives you the option of replacing the duplicate item or skipping it.

Figure 9.54 Backup presents a progress dialog when restoring files from a backup, letting you know which files are being restored.

Deleting Items from the iDisk Backup

If you've backed up files to your iDisk and you'd like to delete them, no problem. Simply open Backup, and in the pop-up menu in the upper left corner of the window choose Restore from iDisk. Next, check the boxes next to the items you want to delete from the online backup. Press Delete, confirm that you actually *want* to delete the backup, and the files are gone.

If you want to nuke the whole lot, you can erase all of the items in your .Mac backup by opening the Backup application and choosing Clear iDisk Backup Folder from the Edit menu. You'll be asked if you really want to go through with it. Click Yes to do the job.

.MAC
TROUBLESHOOTING

The tools included with your .Mac subscription are fairly straightforward and easy to use. For the most part, you shouldn't have any trouble with them. Of course, no software is perfect. Should you run into a problem, Apple offers a wide range of support options that you should find very helpful. You can find some incredible material, for example, at www.apple.com/support/dotmac as well as in the support section of your .Mac account.

While I can't cover every possible problem that will have you tearing out your hair, I can offer a few solutions to the more common—and vexing—issues you may encounter. In this chapter, I'll help you resolve a few frustrating login problems and iDisk issues, as well as offer some tips on using .Mac support.

I Can't Log In to Some Part of .Mac

Perhaps your Webmail account isn't working properly. Perhaps you've tried to get into your account and can't seem to make it work. Perhaps your iDisk has become inaccessible. Occasionally, whatever the reason, something will go wrong with your .Mac login, and you won't be able to access parts of your account. To make matters worse, you might keep getting error messages that say something like "The service isn't available"—not too helpful.

To resolve a login problem, there are a few things you can try.

◆ First, take a deep breath and walk away from your computer for a few minutes. Your .Mac password may be rejected temporarily if the mail servers are offline for maintenance. A little patience could cure this problem entirely.

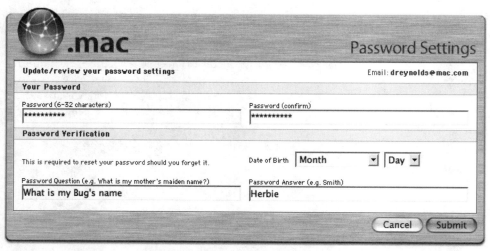

Figure 10.1 By typing your password twice in this dialog, you ensure that the password to which you're changing is spelled correctly. Imagine if you didn't have to confirm the password and you misspelled it— you'd be locked out either until you guessed your misspelling or your password was reset.

Figure 10.2 Apple's password-recovery mechanism lets you retrieve a forgotten password. This page asks for your Apple ID—that's your .Mac e-mail address.

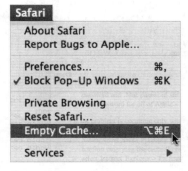

Figure 10.3 To empty Safari's cache, choose Empty Cache from the Safari menu. A browser cache is simply a file (or bunch of files) on your hard drive that a Web browser uses to speed up browsing.

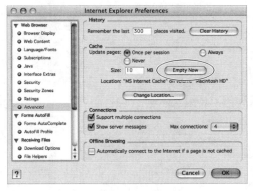

Figure 10.4 Microsoft Internet Explorer allows you to empty its meager 10 MB cache by clicking the Empty Now button in the Cache section. This may resolve some troubles with Web pages, including .Mac pages.

◆ If you don't want to wait or if waiting hasn't helped, you'll want to reset your .Mac password. To do this, log in to your .Mac account using a Web browser, and click the Account link in the lower left area of the homepage to open the Account Settings page. On the Account Settings page, click the Password Settings button. There, you can type a new password. You'll have to enter the password twice: once in the Password field and once in the Password (confirm) field (**Figure 10.1**). Once done, click Submit.

◆ Can't remember your password? Go to http://iforgot.apple.com, where you can reset your AppleConnect password (**Figure 10.2**). Since your AppleConnect password and .Mac password are the same, do note that resetting this will reset your password for *all* of Apple's services. For complete instructions on how to do this, head to Apple's support page at http://docs.info.apple.com/article.html?artnum=86395.

◆ If the problem is occurring only when you use your Web browser to access .Mac services, then you may need to empty the browser's cache. To do this with Safari, select Safari > Empty Cache (Command-Option-E) (**Figure 10.3**). With Microsoft Internet Explorer for the Mac, select Explorer > Preferences, and then select the Web Browser > Advanced category. Click the Empty Now button in the Cache area of the window, and then click OK (**Figure 10.4**).

My iDisk Free Space Is Wrong

Sometimes the amount of space available on your iDisk isn't correct—either you should have more than your iDisk says you do, or you should have *less* than your iDisk says you do. If you're confronting either of these situations, you can do something about it.

To correct your reported iDisk free space, try the following:

◆ Wait a while. If you wait 24 hours or so—especially if you maintain a local copy of your iDisk or you've just upgraded your iDisk storage—the problem may correct itself. Sometimes it takes a while for these changes to take effect, or a hiccup on the server may cause the wrong disk size to be shown. If the problem hasn't corrected itself after a day or so, it's time to try something new.

◆ Try unmounting your iDisk by dragging it to the Trash, and then remounting it (see Chapter 3, "Using iDisk"), which may force the disk size to be represented properly. If that doesn't work, try unmounting your iDisk, restarting your Mac, and then remounting it.

◆ If you're maintaining a local copy of your iDisk, try turning off iDisk synchronization. To do this, open Apple menu > System Preferences and click the .Mac icon. Make sure the iDisk tab is selected. Next, click the Stop button in the iDisk Syncing On section (**Figure 10.5**). Wait until your iDisk shows the proper size, and then turn synchronization back on. This should also take care of cases where you receive a message that your local and remote iDisks are different sizes.

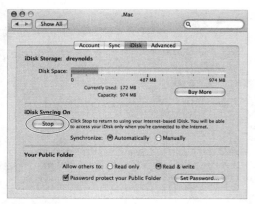

Figure 10.5 A click of the Stop button turns off iDisk synchronization. In Mac OS X 10.4, it'll also leave you with a disk image on your Desktop that contains the contents of your iDisk, which is an easy way to create a backup of your entire iDisk.

```
● ● ●              Terminal — bash — 80x24
Div:/Volumes/iDisk dreynolds$ cd /Volumes/iDisk
Div:/Volumes/iDisk dreynolds$ ls -la█
```

Figure 10.6 Although it looks like near-gibberish to the uninitiated, these two Terminal commands merely move you to your iDisk and then list all of its files (visible and invisible) as shown in Figure 10.7.

```
● ● ●              Terminal — bash — 80x24
Div:~ dreynolds$ cd /Volumes/iDisk
Div:/Volumes/iDisk dreynolds$ ls -la
total 182712
dr-x------   20 dreynold  dreynold        782 May 11 06:09 .
drwxrwxrwt    4 root      admin           136 May 11 05:14 ..
-rwxrwxrwx    1 dreynold  dreynold       6148 May  9 17:44 .DS_Store
drwxrwxrwx    2 dreynold  dreynold         68 Feb 28 14:25 .Groups
drw-------    7 dreynold  dreynold        238 May  9 21:10 .Spotlight-V100
d-wx-wx-wt    3 dreynold  dreynold        102 May 11 05:14 .Trashes
-rw-r--r--    1 dreynold  dreynold   93499392 May 10 10:57 .filler.idsff
-rwxrwxrwx    1 dreynold  dreynold      29087 Apr 29 11:35 About your iDisk.rtf
-rw-r--r--    1 dreynold  dreynold          0 May 11 06:09 Backup
-rw-r--r--    1 dreynold  dreynold       1024 May 10 15:19 Desktop DB
-rw-r--r--    1 dreynold  dreynold          2 May 10 10:54 Desktop DF
drwxrwxrwx    2 dreynold  dreynold         68 May  6 15:16 Documents
-rw-r--r--    1 dreynold  dreynold          0 May 11 06:09 Library
drwxrwxrwx    4 dreynold  dreynold        136 Feb 28 14:25 Movies
drwxrwxrwx    2 dreynold  dreynold         68 Feb 28 14:25 Music
drwxrwxrwx   33 dreynold  dreynold       1122 May  9 18:50 Pictures
drwxrwxrwx    3 dreynold  dreynold        102 Mar 14 19:37 Public
drwxrwxrwx   29 dreynold  dreynold        986 May  7 17:54 Sites
-rw-r--r--    1 dreynold  dreynold          0 May 11 06:09 Software
drwxrwxrwx    4 dreynold  dreynold        136 Apr 13 15:35 Temporary Items
Div:/Volumes/iDisk dreynolds$ █
```

Figure 10.7 Well, who knew all this stuff was on an iDisk? Nothing here is amiss, though, so if we're looking for space savings, we'll have to look elsewhere.

◆ If you're comfortable using Terminal, you can use it to hunt for invisible files that may be using space you don't know about. (You can use the Get Info command when selecting folders in your iDisk to see if folders are larger than they should be.) To look for invisible files, open Terminal (in Applications > Utilities), and type the following, with each line followed by a return (and replace YouriDiskName with the name of your iDisk, typically iDisk), as shown in **Figure 10.6**:

```
cd /Volumes/YouriDiskName
ls -la
```

So, what's going on here (**Figure 10.7**)? The `cd` command changes your present working directory to /Volumes/iDisk (or whatever your iDisk name is). The `ls` command lists the files in the iDisk's root level. In the `-la` flags (which are `l` and `a`), the `l` flag shows the long version of the file listing, and the `a` flag shows all files—even invisible ones. Use the file listing to look for files that don't belong, and delete them.

✔ Tip

■ Do not perform this task if you do not feel comfortable using Terminal to perform basic file manipulations.

I Can't Connect to My iDisk

There are a few things that can cause trouble when connecting to your iDisk—from failed connections to somewhat obscure errors with descriptions consisting almost entirely of a negative number.

To troubleshoot iDisk connection problems, try the following:

◆ If you're using Windows (98, 2000, or XP) to access your iDisk and you're having problems, try restarting your PC. If that doesn't help, remove and then re-create the iDisk connection (see Chapter 3). You might also try using a more expanded URL by ensuring that the URL has a /? (slash followed by a question mark) at the end. For example, instead of `http://idisk.mac.com/yourmembername`, try `http://idisk.mac.com/yourmembername/?`.

◆ Get a faster Internet connection. iDisk works much better with a high-speed Internet connection (as do a lot of other things). If you're running into iDisk problems, see about a high-speed connection—especially with a higher upload speed.

◆ Proxy servers can cause all kinds of connection problems. For example, iDisk Utility for Windows XP will not work with a proxy server, so you'll have to use Network Places. If you're still having problems, ask your ISP if it uses proxy servers, and if so, find out if those servers support WebDAV connections. If they don't, you'll have trouble connecting to your .Mac account. Your ISP may be willing to find a way around the proxy server for you.

◆ If you're getting a -36 error (which is a WebDAV error), make sure you're running the latest version of Mac OS X. If that doesn't solve the problem, then a proxy server may be at issue. Ask your ISP if it uses them and see if your ISP is willing to help you find a way around the proxy server. Also, try a faster Internet connection. This can help solve -36 errors.

◆ If you're getting a -38 error when you try to do something with your iDisk, odds are you're trying to change a file or folder that your iDisk needs in order to work properly. If you're trying to change iPhoto or HomePage files (in the Pictures or Sites folder) on your disk when you see this error, use iPhoto or the HomePage portion of the .Mac Web site to change them instead of doing it through the Finder. If you try to rename a file that HomePage needs to display a Web page, for example, you may see this error.

◆ If your iDisk password is longer than eight characters and you're using iDisk Utility for Windows XP, use only the first eight characters of your password. iDisk Utility for Windows XP doesn't support the longer passwords.

What Is WebDAV, Anyway?

Thought you'd *never* ask! WebDAV is a way of using the HTTP protocol (which is merely the way your computer requests and loads Web pages) for something it wasn't intended for: moving files over the Internet.

WebDAV, which stands for Web-based Distributed Authoring, was originally intended to provide a way to read pages with a Web browser as well as edit them. Often these days, WebDAV is used to handle moving files to and from remote storage volumes, such as an iDisk.

A great place to find out more about WebDAV is at the WebDAV FAQ (www.webdav.org/other/faq.html).

What Is a Proxy Server?

Proxy servers allow computers to make indirect connections to the Internet (or other networks). A proxy server works like an intermediary middleman—that is, users request a connection (such as for a Web page) from the proxy server, and the proxy server goes out and finds that file, grabs it, and then returns it to the user who requested it.

Proxy servers do the following:

◆ Provide additional network security for users (because bad guys have to break in through the proxy server first before reaching a user's computer)

◆ Provide control over what users can see (by blocking requests for certain Web pages or other resources)

◆ Help speed up browsing (by keeping local copies of frequently fetched files that can be loaded by users much faster than if they had to be retrieved over the Internet)

If you're working with a broadband router that relies on NAT (Network Address Translation), you're using a kind of proxy. Many ISPs use proxy servers to help speed up the customer browsing experience.

Proxy servers, though, can sometimes cause unexpected problems, such as breaking large file downloads or causing problems with some Internet services, such as VPN or .Mac.

Curious about proxies? Visit the Wikipedia article at http://en.wikipedia.org/wiki/Proxy_server.

Using .Mac Support

Your .Mac account includes a complete support section to help you get the most out of your .Mac account. It's also a great place to go if you're having a problem with your .Mac account and you don't know where to get the answer. The .Mac support area has a number of features worth investigating (even if you're not having troubles).

To get to your .Mac support materials, log in to your .Mac account and click the Support link on the left side of the page. This takes you to the main support page, which lists a series of help topics, as well as a sidebar full of useful links.

In the main help area, you can find assistance with the following:

◆ .Mac Mail

◆ iDisk

◆ HomePage

◆ .Mac and Mac OS X applications (iPhoto, iMovie, iCal, Address Book, Safari, and iSync)

To access any of these help topics, click the headline above the description. This loads a page of frequently asked questions on the selected topic. At the bottom of the page you'll find an e-mail form that you can use to ask questions of .Mac staffers, who will try to get you an answer within 24 hours.

(continues on next page)

USING .MAC SUPPORT

The sidebar along the left side of the page has a series of links to other useful resources, including:

◆ A search engine that looks through Apple's support Knowledge Base

◆ At-a-glance indicators that show the current status of the .Mac network, .Mac e-mail, iDisk, and HomePage (a green circle is good)

◆ A link to the .Mac discussion boards, which are part of the larger Apple support discussion boards

◆ A link to the "Getting Started with .Mac" PDF, which is worth downloading

◆ A link to the .Mac feedback form, in which you can sound off about .Mac

INDEX

INDEX

INDEX